# PIECES *of* GLASS

# PIECES *of* GLASS

*a moment of* tragedy,
*a lifetime of* faith

*Sarah Kay*

**ZONDERVAN®**

**GRAND RAPIDS, MICHIGAN 49530 USA**

ZONDERVAN.COM/
AUTHOR**TRACKER**

# ZONDERVAN®

*Pieces of Glass*
Copyright © 2006 by Sarah Kay Ndjerareou

Requests for information should be addressed to:

Zondervan, *Grand Rapids, Michigan 49530*

---

**Library of Congress Cataloging-in-Publication Data**

Kay, Sarah.
    Pieces of glass : a moment of tragedy, a lifetime of faith / Sarah Kay.
      p. cm.
    Includes bibliographical references.
    ISBN-10: 0-310-26959-8
    ISBN-13: 978-0-310-26959-5
    1. Suffering—Religious aspects—Christianity. 2. Consolation. 3. Kay,
Sarah, 1980– I. Title.
    BV4909.K39 2006
    248.8' 66—dc22

                                   2006003804

---

The following story is told from my perspective. In order to protect the privacy of others involved, some names have been changed.

*Interior design by Michelle Espinoza*

*Printed in the United States of America*

---

06 07 08 09 10 11 12 • 18 17 16 15 14 13 12 11 10 9 8 7 6 5 4 3 2

*For my family who gave me wings*
*And the Olsons who gave me their love*

# CONTENTS

# SHATTERED PIECES

*In* one moment, one single moment, a sledgehammer splintered my existence.

It lay at my feet, a heap of glass—blood and memories in fragmented images, never to be whole again. I had no idea at the time how difficult it would be to see my life so broken and battered. All my strength couldn't have prepared me for this reality. I had never realized the cords of my life were so fragile. The fractures separated me from the world and from breath itself.

Broken wings …

Broken heart …

The words on these pages are pieces of my pain and my steps toward healing. This is my offering of hope and survival to those who find themselves on a similar path.

> *"I know that you can do all things;*
> *no purpose of yours can be thwarted.*
> *You asked, 'Who is this that obscures my plans without*
> *knowledge?'*
> *Surely I spoke of things I did not understand, things too*
> *wonderful for me to know."*
>
> Job 42:2–3

Chapter 1

# TABLE *for* ONE

*No one ever told me that grief felt so like fear.*
C. S. Lewis

*A* moment, a slight hesitation, my hand resting on the knob —and then resolutely crossing the threshold into the funky ambiance of the quiet café, I stand nervously, stomping snow from my black suede boots and trying to shrug off the chill. Winter seems to enjoy tormenting Chicago.

I impulsively decided on this little indulgence after an ironic experience in an eclectic bookshop. Perusing colorful storylines on the backs of book jackets, I realized that none of them could possibly be as dramatic as my life to date. Then sadly, I also realized I could never find the ending of my story from the safety of an armchair.

The waiter, who has the look of one who lives in a sparsely furnished studio apartment thick with art paraphernalia, and who reluctantly mingles with commoners like me, asks that terrifying question: "Table for one?" I nod silently, mildly surprised by the ease with which I do it. Perhaps my newfound courage is due to the season's first coat of snow blanketing the streets and quieting my world for a moment.

So here I am sipping my buttery glass of wine, thinking I am brave and noble. I open my new book, my shield protecting me from this newly imposed condition—eating alone in public. As a woman who had painstakingly avoided such an engagement in the past, I try to get lost in a new fictional world. My mind wanders, but book, wine, the eclectic atmosphere—all of it steadies me as I toe the wire of my comfort zone.

I have always been more comfortable with daredevil acts than with the everyday nuances of life. Let me jump out of a plane, speak in front of a roomful of strangers, even trek across Siberia. These were the kinds of experiences that defined my life—until now. Now the thought of lounging in public by myself without the faintest possibility of meeting someone seems daunting.

But I have no one to meet. I am a stranger here, and most of the time I take comfort in the anonymity. I grew up in an ever-changing kaleidoscope of strange cities, sights, and smells. Being in the unknown is more familiar than the broken reality I have left behind.

Every new corner, coffee house, and boutique is the sweetest intimacy for my bruised soul. Simple interactions with shopkeepers and neighbors have sustained me and sheltered me from real life. Here I am free from the sympathetic looks of acquaintances, from run-ins with old high school friends that turn awkward when the curious person asks, "So what's new with you?"

The innocence of that question assumes that we all faithfully move on in predictable normalcy—marriage, job, kids. Not me. I am somehow on the other side of the looking glass, a voyeur into life. But that's not quite accurate either. I am living, but it's a life that doesn't seem real.

I hardly recognize myself. This person I look at through the mirror is fragile, yet I feel solid inside. Some strange substance is filling up my soul, as if the ache inside me is taking up all the space where my heart should be. Daily proof that I am being changed on a biological level, as if my very DNA were being rewritten; it is the pain that is so much more than pain. Not just a feeling or an emotion that ebbs and flows, it is tangible. Strong, yet soft. Heavy, yet malleable. Something like gold, refined by suffering. I now understand how the term "heart of gold" could evolve into such a compliment. It's difficult not to appear a saint when you wear a cross of suffering in your eyes and when your compassion is so easily tapped into. From afar, I'm sure it seems like there is a perpetual halo around me. I feel like a stranger could brush me on the street and a chunk of my soul would break off. I wonder if I will hear the wind whistle through the holes. Like a skeleton, I teeter down the street on dry bones.

≈ ≈

Most days it feels as if the world is whirling around me and I am standing still. In slow motion I watch the colors blur; people and faces all become a massive wash. Time crawls on, minute by minute, as sheer exhaustion and fear grip my insides. I am trapped within the whirlwind and have no idea when it will stop. Not long ago I had been full of dreams, when the world was friendly and I was raring for adventure and responsibility. Now I long for any reason to get off this dizzying reality.

≈ ≈

This is my fate, my life; there is no denying my twisted existence, so I have banished myself to this new territory. A few weeks ago I wandered into the quaint little village of Oak Park. A turn-of-the-century suburb, it has an El-stop and several Bohemian hangouts, which qualifies it as urban enough for me. Frank Lloyd

Wright left his mark on the place, and the hometown boy Ernest Hemingway attracted a cultured crowd. The sights are cozy-eclectic and the people interesting—a requisite for my newly built lifestyle. I intend to spend my time in the safety of watching, not in the risk of doing.

I have a few comforts. A single bed, a recliner, and a table are all I have to show for myself, but I have high hopes for the warm, spacious rooms and the lovely French doors. My antique apartment looks like something out of a movie, and it wooed me the moment I walked in the door, footsteps echoing across the beautiful hardwood floors. The ten-foot ceilings graced with crown molding and sconces are more than this recent college graduate could dream of. At the moment it's an odd match for my college furniture, but it's the first thing I've been excited about since the accident. Here there is hope as I wander out into the world alone. If I can make something beautiful out of my home, then maybe, just maybe, there's hope for the rest of life as well.

～ ～

In my new little world my friends are the man who sells me coffee and the woman who sells me shoes. My conversations happen at the movies when the young worker with mental challenges takes my ticket and says, "Hello, Supermodel!" How quickly this becomes the highlight of my week. These friendships are simple. I get everything I need—a smile, a bit of kindness, a latte—and I walk away feeling like I'm normal. Some days I wander the hardware store for odds and ends of decorating supplies that I will somehow incorporate into my haven. It seems the deeper I sink into despair, the more the creativity flows from my hands. Wine bottles become lamps and copper wires flow into ornaments. Like a leftover person, I haunt the library, the grocery store, bookshops, the park. I am quickly becoming a recluse, but everything I need is in a four-block radius and it feels so good to insulate myself from the world.

⁂

Moving away from home and family to take a job where I never have to leave my house was a drastic step. But it feels like the answer to my existence. Back home no one knew what to say to me, and I certainly didn't know what to say to them. My pain felt like a burden; my presence felt like a specter of the past. So I left. I jumped at the first chance for independence, to have my own private corner of the world.

Most days I can be found in a pair of fuzzy white slippers with hopeful red hearts on them, shuffling around on the gleaming hardwood, a cup of coffee in one hand and a pair of reading glasses perched on my nose or nestled beside the pencils in my curly auburn hair. Working in a "virtual office" is, I imagine, somewhat comparable to being under house arrest. With proper food supplies and a cordless headset permanently attached to my ear, I can go for days without seeing another human being—unless you count "the belly." This permanently shirtless fellow lives across the alley and keeps his blinds above chest level. As familiar as I am with his naval, I could walk right past him on the street and never recognize him.

Twenty-two years old and acting like an old maid, I make up names for my neighbors. I listen to talk radio when I need to hear a human voice. I even call in when I'm especially lonely. The friends I invite into my home and hang out with during lunch are Oswald Chambers, Elisabeth Elliot, C. S. Lewis, Beth Moore, Dan Allendar, Annie Lamotte, Donald Miller. I suppose it's only natural that I have started writing, as if to finish the other half of the conversation. In the absence of people, I talk with my hands.

Laughter from the other side of the restaurant snaps me out of my reverie, and I blink, trying to get my bearings. My dinner, half-forgotten, reminds me that it's getting late. As I stand, I catch my reflection in the now darkened window. Not tall, not short, dark hair, olive skin—I could be anyone; my ethnicity could be partly anything. But the curvaceous shape, well, that's from my grandmother. I'm not just anyone. Many strong women make up the image in the mirror—a long line of pioneer women and missionary matriarchs who endured life and persevered in faith. I wonder if survival is found in a gene.

I pay my bill, gather my coat around me, and leave the rosy glow of the café, tucking my chin into the deep folds of my scarf. The snow has stopped falling and lies thick across the city.

My thin boots are no match for the wet snow as I gingerly maneuver into used footsteps already stamped into the newly fallen whiteness. "Oh, great," I groan as I reach my car that is sitting beneath a pile of fresh snow. No gloves, no window scraper—I am definitely not ready for winter, but pulling my hand inside my jacket, I clumsily begin to sweep the snow from the car, leaving most of it sticking to my pants.

"I wasn't born for this," I mutter under my breath. My first memories are of warm yellow heat beating down on my suntanned back, the smell of salt air pungent around me as I dig into the coarse sand at my feet. In these visions, my arms stick out from my body, held in place by two orange plastic water wings that squeak to remind me I have been out of the water too long. The shores of the French Riviera seem far removed from my current locale. As missionaries with Trans World Radio, my parents took three-year-old me to Monaco for the summer while my father, an electronics engineer, assisted them with their radio ministry. Morning glories opened their royal purple faces to drink in the Mediterranean sun, the smell of salty air mixed with fresh baked bread, and the steep cobbled streets wound up the mountainside. We lived on the outer border of Monte Carlo, one of the wealthiest kingdoms in the world, across the street from France. In the morning the French chickens woke us in the Monaco penthouse of our urban apartment.

From the knee level of my parents I took in the sights: French flowers, food, chickens, Roman ruins, even Jacqueline Kennedy Onassis (or at least her yacht). Once a Rolls-Royce parked outside our apartment for weeks because it had a flat tire. Another time I was eating an ice-cream cone while my mother was rescuing the drips that were running down the side of the cone and threatening to grime me. Out of the corner of her eye she realized a man was trying to take a picture and hurried me out of the way. "Well, actually, I was trying to take a picture of her," the man confessed. He photographed for *National Geographic* and had been stationed in our picturesque environs for weeks.

On Friday nights, all the missionaries would go to the beach. Most of the locals and jet-setting tourists were at the world-renowned casino, the sidewalk cafés, and the other French night-haunts. In a city known for its exotic and expensive nightlife, missionaries didn't fit the norm. At night the beaches cleared out and most of the topless bathers disappeared to other activities, so the missionaries dared to go out on the sand with their families. On Fridays they spent the evening picnicking near the jetty where the biggest and best nightclub glittered and the roof of the casino opened to the stars. On one particular evening the sounds of Frank Sinatra could be heard, the *real* Frank, crooning to the swank crowd with a band of missionaries eavesdropping by the water.

Saturday nights in the summer, fireworks companies from around the world competed for the privilege of hosting Prince Rainier's birthday display the following February. The lights were so bright you had to shade your eyes, and the sounds were nearly deafening. I stood at the harbor smelling the gunpowder and feeling the explosions thudding against my chest as we oohed and aahed.

Monte Carlo was my first interaction with missionaries, a career to which my parents aspired. It was also my first interaction with God, or at least God's hand in history. The real reason this little band of believers had landed in such a hedonistic spot on the map was actually due to Hitler.

At the end of World War II, Hitler had built himself a giant radio transmitter on the edge of the Mediterranean to transmit his propaganda all over the world. He was convinced that the world would follow him if they could but hear his voice and understand his grand design. As the story goes, the Germans languished and Hitler was hiding in his bunker, hounding his engineers to get the station operational. Finally, in an attempt to placate the führer, an engineer mocked a small dummy signal a few miles from the bunker so Hitler could hear it on his radio there in the heart of Berlin, appeasing him and getting him off their backs. Hitler went to his death believing the signal was finally on the air.

The huge station was just nearing completion when the war ended, and it sat fully equipped, never having been turned on. Although the station was in France, the French decided they didn't need it and deeded it to Monaco, its nearest neighbor. As one of the smallest principalities in the world, Monaco used it only minimally — its incredible potential unachieved for the most part.

After the war, about half of Europe fell into the hands of the Russians, eventually falling behind the Iron Curtain where atheism was taught and Christianity fell under strict state supervision. The

Russian leaders closed churches and persecuted Christians. Behind the curtain, religious training became nearly impossible.

Finally an American pastor approached the principality of Monaco, asking for permission to use the huge transmitter and its many radio frequency bands. A deal was struck with Prince Rainier, and Trans World Radio began broadcasting the gospel in many languages to Eastern Europe and Russia, to millions of people over the Iron Curtain where missionaries couldn't go.

Personally I was more excited about climbing the ample cherry trees outside the marble structure my parents valued so much, but I couldn't miss the awe in their voices as they worshiped this powerful God who could move dictators and princes on his behalf. I took the message to heart: God used one evil dictator to build a machine that would undermine Lenin and Stalin and all the regime of the USSR. God is a strategist and could even use my parents as integral parts of history. God can use evil to change us, then use *us* in ways we could never imagine.

I was a budding preteen when my awe of God's power grew to an awareness that he was personally invested in my life. I remember when my parents and I were poring over an encyclopedia trying to learn about Swaziland, another tiny kingdom, this one in southern Africa—our next destination with Trans World Radio. I don't know which was more shocking, the topless tribal women in the pictures or the thought of Africa itself. Perhaps every young person hostilely fears the unknown; for me, this mind-set stayed with me as we trekked across half of the known world and landed with a thud on the other half.

No matter what my fears were, rational or otherwise, my father had vision, and I quickly learned that his will could not be easily swayed. However, he did begin to include me in the decision-making conversations of our household and I quickly found my voice, thrilled also to discover my father's interested ear.

Swaziland was exotic but the primitiveness accosted my tender senses. The adjustments to my new surroundings were hardest on all of us at Christmastime. In the Southern Hemisphere December means summer, and this was just too difficult to get used to. I wanted a white Christmas! One hot and sunny Christmas Eve, I was grumpy and frustrated. I stomped my foot and shot an angry prayer to God. I figured since he had gotten us into this mess, then he should do something about it!

"God," I pouted, "why can't you make it feel more like home?"

Within seconds a huge gust of wind poured through our open windows, bringing our Christmas tree crashing down on the parquet floor, followed by a roar of cold rain pounding our tin roof. Immediately my family all rushed into the living room to gather scattered ornaments and right the fallen tree. By the time we had salvaged our Christmas, we found ourselves shoulder to shoulder, staring at the miracle before our eyes. A chill had fallen over the air with the darkened sky, and a hush fell over all of us as we saw the miracle in the backyard. Light sparkled off a crystal clear whiteness that covered the ground like a solid blanket. While we had been scurrying to save our possessions inside, it had hailed outside, covering the backyard with ice. Christmas! It was the first time God had shown up for me. I was duly impressed, and admittedly a little spooked.

That was then. Now, however, the cold clammy snow has lost some of its magic as I brush the last of it off my car and climb inside. Teeth chattering and drenched to the bone, I hunch over in the driver's seat waiting for the heat to defrost my fingers. I don't dare walk the fourteen blocks back to my apartment. Although the neighborhood is handsome, it's late and I'm reminded again that I am alone in the world. Alone and therefore vulnerable, a category that I don't feel prepared for. I guess it's true you want what you cannot have. At times like this I find myself longing for someone to hold me, to keep me safe, and to warm the ice-cold chill of my hands and my heart. I know that some wounds are not meant to be healed by human touch. Only the tears of the Divine can cleanse these smudges on our souls. I know this truth only too well, and yet every night I wrestle, longing for anyone, anything that will make the hurt go away.

Reminders of my independence stalk me, a state that has been forced upon me and threatens to smother any life that still struggles to survive. I am woman. Strong woman, soft woman, deep woman, fiery woman, wounded woman, young woman. The need to love, to nurture, to give, to hold, and to be held—all the things my sex has so tried to claim were androgynous virtues—these are what make me she! My heart screams out in defiance. I know that I'm capable and competent, and people will pay me good money to work for them. But who will love me? I'm attractive and I'm smart and I meet the standards of the role models set before me on TV and on the covers of glossy magazines. I'm young and able, beautiful and capable. But is that all there is?

Yet those things don't keep me up at night. I worry about what type of weapon to carry that will take the place of his strong arm and long shadow. I worry that I will completely lose myself in my working world, that I will never touch the soft part of me again. I wonder who will find delight in my eyes or get lost in my smile. I wonder whose soul I will want to run my fingers through. Can anyone fill the shoes of the man I love?

I wonder why the single life seems like suffering to me. I am not very good at it. Much nobler people make the single life venerable. Why do I long to find my fulfillment in someone else's eyes?

Am I shallow? Am I insecure? I had felt God's presence powerfully while I was in love, like God himself had sent someone to take care of my heart and protect me. Now I have no love, and it seems God is gone too. The faith that has supported me from my earliest memories seems to be sputtering. I feel myself lurching for God, longing for that deep constant awareness of his presence. Like a blind woman in the darkness, I grope but find nothing. "Have you deserted me too, God?" I whisper, afraid to speak the words, afraid to doubt, afraid to admit that my broken heart feels forgotten. My prayer echoes. No one is there and my heart is heavy with loss.

I pull the car into my parking space, grateful that the motion lights flick on to greet me. The harsh light on the white snow seems like the only comfort I have these days. Crossing the street, the shadows fall across my path as the lamplight filters through the massive oak trees that line my avenue. A man with a striped bag asks me for directions. I'm not in the mood for human contact, but I know the answer to his question and blindly oblige, then bend my head to focus on the keys in my hand. My back gate is an ominous metallic door facing the alley that separates two sets of apartments.

Suddenly I am lurched backward by a strong arm pulling at the purse hooked over my shoulder. A face thrusts itself into my line of vision and growls, "Give me your purse!" My mind reels, but not at the words. It's the look of evil that's taken over the man's face, now so close to mine. This can't be happening! No, this can't be happening!

Grabbing my purse with both hands, I react to the evil more than anything, the sick confidence that his will should supersede mine simply by force! At this moment I have no option. I react with the first instinct that comes: anger. *How dare you!*

22

"Noooooo!"

"B****, I'll shoot you." He thrusts me toward the bushes with the arm that was hanging onto my purse, and I see a slim glimmer of light in the other hand.

*That's not a gun*, my head says to my heart, and my hands never even consider letting go. But my mouth knows what to do. "Noooooo! Let go!"

In another instant the words of my Wheaton College self-defense teacher come rushing into my head. She had trained countless missionary women and filled us with amazing stories of ones who were rescued from perilous moments by calling on the name of the Lord for strength.

"Stop in the name of Jesus!" I scream. "STOP in the name of JESUS!"

Suddenly his back is against the wall. The object masquerading as a gun rises in his hand and slams into the top of my head. It's hard and metallic, and it feels like fireworks exploding behind my eyes as I duck for cover, still holding blindly to my bag. One, two, three, four blows to the back of my head. I duck again and begin screaming even louder. My arms strain to hold onto the bag as we circle in a vulgar dance. Five, six, seven, my vision begins to blur, each blow growing stronger and accented by a resounding "Let go, B****!"

My eyes focus on the feet in front of my own and clumsily I kick and kick. My attacker jumps aside, and then, the unthinkable—as we both cling to the beige bag between us, he bends low, hovering over me, and latches onto my upper arm with his teeth. I shriek in terror at the audacity of it all.

I'm falling, smashing against the cement walk, my hands still clinging to my purse with alarming strength. Two more blows to my face shatter my resolve and my will to fight, and then the world goes black.

As my vision comes back into focus, I hear myself sobbing, lying limply on the damp sidewalk. Doors open and gentle arms come running. From all over, my neighbors come to my rescue. Scooping me up and filling me with energetic compassion, a kind man tries to get me to stop sobbing. Still filled with adrenaline and hostility, I find this moronic. I just went three rounds fighting for my life. For heaven's sake, let me cry!

By the end of the evening, and with the help of my shivering band of neighbors, my assailant is found and identified. I even redeem my belongings, though I'm not expecting to touch them any time soon. "Why didn't you just give him your purse?" my worried neighbors gush. I don't even try to explain myself.

The policeman who is escorting me to the station just down the block assures me I did the right thing. "If you hadn't fought, there's no telling what he would have done," he swears, shaking his head.

I hold my head up a little higher. But when I call my mother who is four hours away, all my courage fades.

"Mom, I was attacked!" I blubber into the phone.

"Were you raped?" she asks in a horrified, angry voice.

"No," I answer, finding something to be thankful for. I give an overview of the story, but I don't share all the details. I don't want her to hear the ugly words he threw at me—spoken with hatred as if I deserved the beating, as if the venom raining down on my head was revenge on every person who had ever hurt him. Today fear is the master and the violence has won.

"I am so proud of you," she says, her voice full of emotion and anger.

Midnight phone calls have become all too frequent in my family, and they never bring good news. I reassure her that I have plenty of people taking care of me. I have survived the ugly ordeal and will live to see justice. But it takes days for me to share all the details. The most difficult thing to pull from my mind is the angry voice repeating the ugly words in my head. In fact, at court a few days later, I am compelled by the need to appear calm in order to regain my dignity from this man.

I want to scream, "It was *my* house and *my* things and I am *sorry* for your pain but you had no right to do this! Not here! Not anywhere!"

In the darkness two lives crashed together like two violent halves of a torrid yin and yang. Out of violence, both merely survive, two people bound together in a grotesque moment. But starkly juxtaposed, the true natures exposed themselves. As he threw down his vile words with dehumanizing intent, I reached for the only power I knew that could protect my body, mind, and soul. Later I found out that my attacker had also robbed two men with his makeshift metal gun on the same day. I get some relief when he is sentenced to twelve years for aggravated assault and robbery, but I have even more solace from the thought that it took a woman and the name of Jesus to bring this man down.

I guess there is still some fight left in me. In fact, I know if it wasn't for the terrible events earlier in the year, I probably would have caved, but pain has brought anger, and righteous anger was exactly what I needed that night.

Chapter 2

# CHEST PAINS

*The Lord gives us only what we can handle;*
*I just wish he didn't think I could handle so much.*
Mother Teresa

*T*he traffic slows to a crawl and the city rolls past my frosty window. My good intentions are melting by the mile. I know what I should do. The words of Paul Simon enter my brain like poison: "Losing love is like a window in your heart. Everyone knows you're torn apart. Everyone sees the wind blow."[1]

The closer I get to my house, the more trapped I feel. Trapped in a life of pain, forgetfulness, independence, and responsibility. The pounding in my chest beats deeper into my heart and sears with pain. I try to get it under control—*I'm not doing that again.*

Four days ago I thought I was having a heart attack. Either that or I was going crazy. I couldn't breathe and I woke up with what felt like an elephant sitting on my chest. My doctor's office allowed an emergency appointment, but it took all my restraint to keep from throwing my shoe at the doctor when he tried to stick me in the hospital for tests. My mind screamed at him—*Don't you understand? How stupid are you? I am stressed out because of what a hospital*

1. Paul Simon, "Graceland" *Graceland*, Warner Bros./WEA, 1986.

*has done, or has failed to do, so why would I want to go back?*—and with all the adrenaline in my system, I almost let loose. I felt like it was his fault and the fault of all the ignorant people in white coats who believed that they and only they had the answers. How could someone with that much education and intelligence be so ignorant? And why did he stare at me like I was crazy? After all this, I would have been better off crazy. Then I would have an excuse for this visit. I knew that this young doctor didn't know me and didn't want to know of my troubles. He didn't want to give a young girl Valium, fearful that I'd become addicted. If he was anyone I trusted, I could gently tell my story and let him see the truth. Denial is always simpler and often gentler, at least for a while. If it weren't the truth, it would have felt better.

The truth was that I had kept my mind and my faith in the middle of a living hell, but now in its aftermath, I was stuck, unmoving. Those months I had sat by Paul's side in the hospital, I could summon the forces of my soul to be calm, surrounded by the rhythm of machines and beeps. *Be strong for him*, I told myself. *He needs you to be strong*, I reminded myself over and over.

I had often looked at the pain-stricken faces of loved ones in the waiting room. So much heartache and no end in sight. Hope had been stripped from these people, and no one knew what to say to me. *Be strong for them.* Every minute of every day, it nearly broke me that I couldn't offer them anything.

My mother had taught me that consequences for attitude are no less real than for action. That thought allowed me to hold my head high, to move forward with purpose, to finish my final semester of college, traveling back and forth between classes and the hospital. I was a fighter. The only thing I had to offer those who loved me was my strength. Surrounded by them I was fortified and safe.

But it's more difficult to stay calm when the winds are howling in your head instead of in some hospital room. I had moved away from the safety of my parents' home, and silence suddenly filled my life. In secluding myself from others to protect them from my pain, my emotions had broken out of control.

☙ ❧

I climb the steps to my apartment and crawl under the blankets on my couch. Here in the silence of my new life the storm in my soul screams and rages as if getting its revenge from months of suppression. I lie flat on my back as if I've reached my physical limit for solitude. The emotions that I have been suppressing are inescapable. I am hurting, hurting so deeply I can't even process the weight of it. No relief is in sight. All I see in store for me is pain, and I think I'll go insane.

I wait for it to pass, but it doesn't. Frustrated and scared, I call the doctor's office.

"My dear, you need to de-stress," the kind and personal doctor tells me as I sit on the table in front of her. I'm embarrassed because it's my second visit this week. I'm glad it's a different doctor. "Your body is processing the emotions that you're suppressing and you have only a couple of choices. Have you ever heard of post-traumatic depression?"

"Depression? I always thought depression was weeping and crying, always feeling blue?" I ask, incredulously.

"Well it can be, but there are several lesser-known symptoms connected to cognitive thought. These may be affecting your ability to organize and problem solve."

"Well I admit, I feel like a wreck." I sigh deeply, considering the past few months. "I've just been so tired and I keep forgetting to do necessary things like buying groceries, doing laundry, paying bills. I feel like I'm half a person. But I thought that was just the reality of my situation, you know, learning to live without Paul."

The kind doctor smiles sympathetically and I begin to confess my inner insanity. "Even when I go to church, I'm as fragile as glass. When I try to make the simplest decision, I find myself muddled and confused, like there's some short in my system. I make a decision, but I can't describe how I feel about it for weeks; then the feelings come, and two weeks after that I finally have the rationale for why I made my original decision. Six weeks is a long time to doubt yourself, especially when you can't seem to explain your actions to the ones you love." I look at the doctor and realize I have begun to cry.

"Worst of all, I don't know where to turn for wisdom or comfort," I stammer breathlessly. "I just know I'm alone—mind, body, and soul. And I am so fragile that the least bit of indifference from anyone is, well, so jarring that it feels like heartbreak or treason. You know, I've been turned down by two support groups," I admit dryly, laughing at the absurdity of it all. I'm caught between realities because I don't fit their criteria. My fiancé isn't actually dead so I can't take solace with widowed spouses, and since he isn't actually my spouse, I don't fit into the 'Spouses of Brain Injury Victims' group.

"Now you're telling me the pain in my heart is seeping into my body like a poison? And I just thought I was going crazy," I say with a weak smile.

In a way, I'm glad for her diagnosis. I've been frustrated by my inability to function. I haven't understood where grief ends and insanity begins. It seems crazy that the simplest tasks are daunting and overwhelming to me, when before I had somehow managed to have so much strength and dignity. I had always relied on two things, God's faithfulness and my almost impeccable instincts. Now everything is gone, but at least I'm beginning to understand why.

The doctor interrupts my thoughts. "Can you tell me more about Paul?"

The question hangs in the air as if I could flick it with my forefinger and watch it clatter to the floor. But I have no answer.

*Please don't ask me that.*

She waits.

Those memories are sealed away so deeply that I believe my heart will break if I try to touch his face in my mind. Honestly, I don't know what's worse, remembering or failing to. I realize with a moment of panic that I cannot find him in my mind. Has my survival cost me the face of my dearest love?

Now in a single moment and from a scrap of conversation, a watery scene materializes before my eyes. I see him standing at the first-floor window, hands on the sill, a sandal-clad foot leaning on a piece of concrete. In the same moment, I hear the mellow sound of his voice.

"The whole baked potato in my mouth! You should have seen the look on his face!" He throws back his head to revel in his own humor. It's all there—the sound of his laughter, the pace of his words, his spiky hair, and his lean brown shoulders that stooped ever so slightly. He is here, as if I am watching him this very moment.

I feel a tear wet my cheek and, just as mysteriously as the scene arose, it is gone from my eyes. But the presence of that moment continues to warm my heart even as I brush the tears from my eyes. For now it is enough to hear his warm laughter in my ears. It is enough to know that he is still here, the best part of me.

The doctor sits on her stool, clipboard in hand, and I tell my story as if for the first time.

🐟 🐟

The weather had been warm for February and we traveled far north to find a place that still had snow for skiing. Paul loved the snow. Some of his most amazing experiences with the Lord had been in the rugged wilderness of northern Wisconsin. The Olson men would meet regularly for a romp in the woods that they tried to pass off as hunting. I believe Paul cared more for the time with family in the untouched majesty of "God's country" than whether he brought home a deer. No matter how competitive he was about getting a deer, he always was overwhelmed by the Lord's presence in the stillness of the softly falling snow.

This night in February wasn't any different. A church retreat rather than a hunting trip, but Paul was having the time of his life in the outdoors that he loved so much. His wild and fun-loving nature had eaten up the sloping mountains of Wisconsin. He had planned on attending the retreat as a lay-pastor and had begged me to go along. It was four months before our wedding, and I had so much to do. I loved to ski and all my friends were going, but I had loads of homework on top of everything. I called my mom several times, weighing the options.

I was leaning toward staying home, but at the last moment I'd phoned her saying, "Mom, I just can't get it out of my mind that I'm supposed to be there this weekend. I know it doesn't make any sense for me to go, but I just know I *have* to. I think the Lord must have some reason for me to be there." She didn't even try to argue, so I packed my bags and threw myself into the weekend.

Planned activities, praise and worship, and great teaching kept us busy until four o'clock on Saturday afternoon. Then we all headed off for an evening ski run under the lights. As a natural athlete with a competitive spirit, Paul was not going to be left behind, even though this was his first time on skis. Wearing borrowed equipment, he'd been speeding down the slopes ahead of me all afternoon and into the night. We'd chuckled as he'd taken an occasional tumble. When we rode the ski lift together, we talked of future trips we'd take, and how much fun he was having. Once I made him promise that he wouldn't get hurt. As we gently glided down the slopes, we sang our song by the Turtles:

> *The only one for me is you, and you for me*
> *So happy together.*[2]

The hill was closing at 9:00 p.m. and we were taking the last run of the evening. The temperature was dropping from the comfortable 32 degrees we'd been enjoying all day, but we really hadn't noticed the chill. As we neared the crest of the hill, I felt myself trying to say something, and yet my mind couldn't understand why I needed to voice those exact words. But they burst out of my mouth as if I had no control. "Hey! Do you love me?"

Paul slowed, looked over his shoulder and said, "Of course I love you ..."

Those were the last words anyone has ever heard him say.

I watched him ski down a huge bowl-shaped embankment. The run was rated only medium difficulty, and I was smiling as I raced behind him. But as Paul crested the top of the ridge, his six-foot frame leaned toward the edge and his head slammed into a large pole that was holding up a snow fence a few inches behind the crest. His body flew about six feet from the pole and wedged behind the fence and the crest. If I hadn't been watching from behind, I would never have known where he had landed.

When I caught up to him at the base of the hill, I knew something was dreadfully wrong. Blood pooled around his head and poured from his mouth and nose in silence. I took Paul's head in my hands and began to scream, "Help! Help! He's bleeding!"

---

2. The Turtles, "Happy Together," *Happy Together*, Sundazed Music Inc., 1967.

My world ground to a halt. As I watched casual skiers move below us, oblivious to my nightmare, I knew life would never be the same again. When the first help arrived, I was on the edge of hysterics. A woman appeared and took control of the situation. She barked at me to pull myself together and shouted at her husband to get the ski patrol. The only thing I could do was pray. Audibly, I began to talk to God over Paul. I didn't care who heard. In that moment I felt myself stick my faith in the ground like a stake, so sure was I of God's power. This was his territory. Only he could fix this for me now.

Paul coughed and a sick gurgling sound came from his mouth as the stranger took my place and clamped her hands onto his head to keep any possible spinal injury from getting worse. I felt my insides surge and revolt, and then I began to go numb. Paul was in an incredibly altered state and, as if a cloud had passed over my eyes, so was I.

When the ski patrol arrived, it took them only seconds to call for a med-flight helicopter. In morbid alertness, I knew this was a very bad sign, and something in me died. Desperate tears began to stream down my face as I left the ski patrol and stumbled down the rest of the embankment, still wearing my ski boots.

I didn't realize how much emotion was flowing through me until I tried to grab one of Paul's friends and form a full sentence. I wailed something about Paul's accident, and to get our pastor to the patrol office, but my face told the rest of the story. Then I rushed into the ski lodge to turn in my boots and retrieve my belongings before they rushed Paul away from me.

My altered state held an incredible awareness of how my life was shattering while others stared on from their comfortable realities. The nurse's husband, who would become one of the gentlest hands I would meet on that cruel evening, guided me up to the lockers to gather my meager belongings. If Paul was going anywhere, I would be with him; and Jim, my new friend, seemed to understand this determination.

In the middle of the crowded lobby, I desperately tore at my boots and gathered my shoes, sitting on the ground like a small child. In a matter of moments I'd been introduced to a darker corner of life, and as if something clicked into place, so did the darker angry portion of my soul that snapped in frustration at the inane actions of those around me. As if with a flourish, my rose-colored glasses had been torn off, and now there was a little announcer in my head giving a play-by-play of all the ridiculous things we were asked to endure.

At the lockers, poor Jim was trying to explain to a slack-jawed teenager where my skis were and why I needed to leave my boots. I remember the rage that welled up in me as he asked me with a bored look, "Do you at least have your ticket?"

The charming people-pleaser in me vanished. "Do I really need a ticket at a time like this?" the voice in my head roared. Yet my mind was working with intense clarity. With frustration pouring through my veins, I pulled the worthless piece of paper from my pocket and threw it at the stupid boy, along with an extra sock just for good measure. I ran back out into the night to find Paul.

My tearful message must have done the trick, because silhouetted against the bright lights stood our college pastor, as if he were made of stone. Instantly he'd become one of the most somber people I'd ever seen, and it provoked in me an intensity of will and resolve to be even calmer than he was. I think I did this simply because everyone expected me to be much more hysterical. I had discovered a new defiant bone in my body that night, and it seemed like the only thing I had any control over.

In the tiny office of the ski patrol I sat on a worn-out teal bench watching patrollers eat their supper and listening to the grotesque sounds of the med-flight crew trying to get oxygen to Paul's brain. The exercise went on and on. Too long. The police came for questions, and I gave them all the information I knew about what had happened. I turned over a long list of phone numbers for them to call.

Jim seemed to be the only one moving in the same dimension that I was. He gave me a glass of water and sat next to me as if protecting me. I remember thinking about the stark contrast of Jim's calming spirit against the young blonde who had been the first patroller to find us on the hill; she looked up from her supper and remarked that she was amazed at me. "If it had been my fiancé—" I didn't hear the rest. I was overwhelmed by my desire to hurt someone. I don't know where the anger came from or why her stupid comment bothered me so much, but just as if my soul had disconnected from my body, I was processing all these emotions behind the veil of stone that had become my face.

In my spirit I knew that tragedy had just tumbled onto me, but in my naïve little world everything had always righted itself before too much time had passed. Both of these realities were at war deep in my spirit, yet the Lord never impressed upon me a false hope that everything would be alright. Nothing was alright and I knew it.

Someone else called Paul's family, someone who was much more upbeat than I. But I called my mother as I sat listening to an agonizing symphony of medical jargon and noises that would make a dentist cringe. She knew even without me saying much at all. She could hear the intense tightness of my voice that didn't match the terror of my words and, without me saying more than four sentences, she assured me that she would pack the family and they would be there as soon as possible.

Still we waited in the odd little room until a gentleman in a navy blue flight suit beelined to my still frame. "We've got Paul stabilized. Would you like to say something to him before we go?" It was such a tender gesture and his eyes were filled with genuine compassion, but all I could think was that they should be getting him to the hospital. It had taken them fourteen minutes to get oxygen to Paul's brain because of how severely his skull had shattered. I was running out of patience. In a quick motion I kissed what was left of Paul that wasn't wrapped in some medical device and told him I would see him very soon. I didn't cry—I just wanted to get him out of there.

There was no room for me in the helicopter, and I couldn't stand to wait any longer. My pastor directed me to a car, and we began the long drive to the University of Wisconsin Hospital in Madison.

Paul's father, Ken, called me midway into town. He and Mary lived just forty miles from the hospital, and he wanted to be sure I knew where I was going. His tone was light and I knew they had no idea. Perhaps if they had seen the stone-faced expression of my pastor, they would have known. Perhaps if they had heard me say moments earlier that I wanted to marry Paul before he passed away, they would have been afraid.

I burst in through the double doors of the hospital ER as if I were playing a role in a movie. The very first person I saw was Paul's younger brother Peter, only a year and some months his junior. Peter and Paul were always very close, though Peter never had much to say to me. But that didn't matter at this moment. We both shared such love for Paul that I rushed into his arms and began to sob. With the strength of character and compassion that are a testimony to all the Olson men, he wrapped his arms around me and held me as I cried.

His stunned family sat in a little glassed-off room and tried to piece together what had happened. Paul had been rushed past them into the operating room for neurosurgery. His parents stood next to their best friends, a doctor and his wife, as they reached out to hold me. Mary whispered that she just knew it would be alright, and Ken, pastor of an Evangelical Free Church, led us in prayer for the surgeons. Their optimism was contagious and I desperately wanted their hopes to be true. They were a part of my world that hadn't been shattered, and their presence was so uplifting.

My worst fear was that Paul wouldn't live through the night, something I didn't share with them. I tried to believe that the world would right itself again and that everything would be okay. But I did voice my concern to the church staff that poured into the hospital, all still clad in bulky ski gear. "If Paul lives or dies tonight," I said, "he will be a very lucky man." Paul's motto had always been "To live is Christ and to die is gain." I understood the extent of his injuries and that his life was hanging in the balance, but I also understood the foundation of Paul's faith, my faith, that death was not something to be feared. His heart truly longed to be in the presence of God.

&#10086; &#10087;

A silent agony happens when a family is transferred from the ER waiting room to the ICU waiting room; it's as if you have officially been invited into purgatory—and the coffee proves it. The Trauma Life Center, TLC, looks like a cross between an office lounge and a refugee camp. Nothing is comfortable and everyone has been there way too long. In the waiting room time stops functioning the same way it does on the outside. Minutes turn into decades and you can lose entire days in the blink of an eye. In the cold quiet halls of the hospital I tried to reach out for anything that would bring me strength. Several times I found myself in the arms of Peter and his girlfriend, Amy—any distance or resentment between us melted inside the cement walls of the hospital; none of it seemed to matter tonight.

⁓ ⁓

At two in the morning my parents appeared. I could see that their presence jarred the Olsons, who were gradually discovering the horrible reality. Paul had gone into surgery around ten thirty that night.

My folks, Blane and Joan Wollschlager, were only four days away from an exploratory trip to China. They were hoping to return to mission work after a ten-year hiatus in the United States while my brother Dana and I had attended high school. Their plan had been to take two weeks to assist a missionary family with small children as they traveled back to China, help them get settled, then return in a year to join them in ministry. That would give Paul and me time to get married and settled into the Chicago suburbs so that we'd be close to Dana when he arrived at Wheaton for his freshman year, giving him a stable home to visit even if they were living in China. The accident caused them to start their trip a few days early in a hotel room in Madison. And they never made it to China.

⁓ ⁓

Hours of surgery and no news. Finding hope in the face of so much horror became my mission. Amy was my answer.

In fact, this was the first time there had been any warmth between the two of us, and I was so thankful. Amy was already a friend of the family, and that meant she was intimate with each of them, from the youngest to the oldest. I don't think I impressed her on our first meeting. In fact, I know I offended her, but it has taken me years to understand how. I was always trying so hard to please everyone. I guess it was an old habit. Moving every two years as a kid, you learn to make friends fast. But I'm not sure if I made any friends the night we met, at least not with Amy. She had a history with this family. Although her disapproval of me was evident, it was never confronted, so we danced around each other in a stony silence. None of that seemed to matter tonight. When threatened from the outside, suddenly we were family.

Sometime during the night, a bleary-eyed resident sat down with our weary band of family. I tried to manage a brave smile, no matter what I felt.

"I have to tell you it's not good," he began. "Paul was without oxygen to the brain for over fourteen minutes. His skull is cracked in several places, and at the point of impact it shattered so badly that we are unable to recreate it at this moment. Paul's jaw is broken and his retinas were detached in the collision. Unfortunately this is irreparable and causes permanent blindness. Paul also sustained severe damage to the temporal and frontal lobes of his brain. There are two temporal lobes, one on each side of the brain, at about the level of the ears. These lobes allow a person to tell one smell from another and one sound from another. They also help in sorting out new information and are believed to be responsible for short-term memory. This region controls motor skills, language, and personality. Damage interferes with the ability to store new memories. Likewise, the ability to use language, recognize familiar faces, to count, read, and many other higher abilities, are dependent on intact memory functions. Impairments in such basic functions are fundamental to personal identity. Wipe out this part of the brain and the person speaks gibberish. With this type of injury patients typically have considerable changes in personality, but Paul's injuries are so incredibly severe that I feel I have to warn you it is highly unlikely that he will ever be able to speak or walk. In fact, it will be a miracle if he is able to understand his environment and interact intelligibly. I would advise you to consider seriously the life you wish for Paul. You must understand that he will be severely altered and disabled. I am sorry, but the Paul you know is gone."

When the green-garbed man began speaking about organ donation, I haltingly got to my feet. Walking between my parents, we moved toward the corridor; then suddenly everything went black and I crumpled to the ground under the weight of it all. Somehow my parents gathered me up and took me to a nearby hotel.

⌒ ⌒

Light streamed through the open window of the hotel room my parents had found across the street from the hospital. I slowly came to with a moment of ignorant bliss before reality came rushing back. I dreaded opening my eyes, but I hated myself for sleeping at a time like this. I dreaded going to the hospital, but I was also anxious to get there as soon as possible. I didn't know how to pray, but my soul seemed to be screaming.

Then somehow as I lay in that strange bed, God's grace started to pour over me, slowly and quietly. I didn't care what the doctor had said. I believed in miracles. Christianity demands faith, which by definition is believing the unseen. Hope is at the core of everything that matters to me — hope in Christ in this life and the next — and so even though I didn't feel hope, I was committed to hope, and in that commitment I found the strength to get out of bed.

After four hours of fitful sleep we trooped back to the TLC where Paul's family had camped out for the night, only to find

Mary wringing her hands and pacing agitatedly. She had been in Paul's room when he suddenly began gasping for breath and a team of specialists came rushing in. She couldn't stand to see him suffering but pleaded with someone to go in to be with him so there would be someone he loved in the room. But no one had had the stomach to go.

My mom, a dental hygienist, felt she could go in because she was more used to medical settings. It was the first time she had seen Paul since the accident. Both eyes were swollen and black, like two purple plums laid against his face. White bandages swaddled his head and his nose and lips were swollen and disfigured. Monitors beeped and whirred around him and tubes came out of everywhere.

He was flailing and gasping for breath as the first of many complications struck and his lung collapsed. Doctors rushed in to insert a tube into his side to drain, then re-inflate the lung, adding to the multiple incisions and scars that would ultimately mark his body. His life hung in the balance and the awfulness of that fact was finally striking us all in the face like a weighted glove.

A second horrible truth collided as we realized that the injury was only the first of many near fatal calamities Paul would have to survive. The severity of the blow Paul had received not only damaged his skull and eyes. When his brain, accelerating forward at a high rate of speed, was suddenly stopped, the momentum forced the soft brain tissue forward, then slammed it into reverse, banging it with equal force against the back of his head and jarring it from its moorings, like tossing a bowl of Jell-O against a wall. The initial injury damaged the brain irreparably, but the secondary problem was swelling.

Trapped within the confines of the head bones, the injured brain began to swell, increasing the intercranial pressure (ICP) to life threatening levels. The doctors knew this would be the case and had literally removed a piece of Paul's skull to make room for expansion, placing it in the freezer for reattachment in the future when his brain returned to normal size.

Once Paul was stabilized, we met with the head neurosurgeon, a kind, intelligent-looking man who assured us that the previous night's diagnosis had been premature. With something that almost seemed like a scoff, he dismissed it, claiming that Paul was young and strong, and after all, we know so little about the brain, it's hard to say what could happen. We clung on to what we wanted to hear.

That day as I sat by Paul's bedside, the presence of Death was so strong that I was sure I would see it if I looked up. Strangely, even that frightening experience gave me hope and validated my faith. If Death was real, then heaven and hell and God himself were real also.

By the third day we began a vigil of monitoring his ICP, hoping that the swelling alone wouldn't kill him. At first they allowed only one or two of us into his room at a time, and we would pull up a chair and slide our hands into his. He seemed to hang on to them for dear life and we were sure he knew we were there. We spent hours praying at his bedside, reading Scriptures, and singing hymns, all the time with our eyes on the ICP monitor.

In the hospital that day I realized that, even as I leaned on all the people who were loving me, praying for me, and caring for me, I would not find comfort from them. Not really. And neither could I comfort them. We each had to feel the pain of loss. It was hard to watch Paul's parents, his siblings, my parents, and the many other people who loved him go through their grief.

But I made a firm resolution not to fall to despair. God's grace had flooded me, and he wouldn't let me forget how much I had to be thankful for. Most of all, I knew that Paul's love would carry me to the end of my days; he had showered me with more love in a year and a half than most women get in a lifetime. "No matter how he comes out of this," I said, "he can't get rid of me. I know how much he cares and how deeply he loves."

Day Four arrived and I had to accept the fact that everything seemed to be slipping away, no matter how firm my resolutions were. The hospital is an eerie place, and my emotions spiked up and down. One moment I was filled with determined faith, and then suddenly it all came tumbling down. "Today was a tough day but full of hope." I don't know how many times I said that as friends and family came streaming into the hospital room to visit. My words were true, but the repetition sometimes made me feel like a puppet.

Still, I was glad they came. People really loved Paul, and it's because he had invested in them. He would always spend a lot of time with our friends and people from church, but this was especially true just before the accident. Days before we had left for our trip to Wisconsin, he'd called my parents and spoken with each member of my family for a long time. We'd gone to his parents' home twice in the past month. It's like somehow he knew ...

🐦 🐦

Day Five. I was getting to know the hospital jargon and the rhythm of orderlies, nurses, and therapists — all moving in and out like clockwork. This was not information I ever wanted to learn; the hospital was not supposed to be a familiar scene for me. On the other hand, I didn't know enough. Because Paul's injuries were so severe, the staff had been careful what information to share with us, giving us only as much as we could bear. We were so dependent on them all to guide us; it was like a mystery trying to figure out little pieces of the puzzle. We often had no idea what we were facing. Sometimes when I saw the sympathy in their eyes, I wondered if they knew something I didn't, something too terrible for words.

In the hours after the accident, people had been flocking to the hospital—an all-night prayer vigil—people gathering to sing; cards and posters accumulating; friends that Paul hadn't seen in years making special trips to show support, mend old wounds, or hold his hand. The nurses and orderlies commented that they rarely saw reactions like this in the ICU; few families have the courage. And yet as each day went by, I wondered who to trust. I didn't blame the doctors for telling us what we wanted to hear—it would take a lot of guts to give bad news to such a determined and hopeful band of believers. And they really were taking such good care of us.

By Day Six, Paul's ICP had risen to dangerous levels and they put him into a drug-induced coma. They lowered the lighting and strapped electrodes to his head, monitoring his brain activity. He felt warm and looked like he had gained twenty pounds. I knew what his hands would look like when he's forty-five.

Day Seven. Day Eight. Day Nine. Time blurred. Most days I sat next to his bed chatting with whomever came in the room. I was thankful for the support, but visiting was draining—as was trying to make all the visitors feel comfortable. People are awkward in the ICU. Most of the Christians had no problem praying, but they clearly found it hard to know how to talk to Paul. I got discouraged too and didn't feel comfortable talking to him personally in front of others. Instead I read, prayed, and sang.

Maybe I was too hopeful, not caring what the doctors' tests said he could and couldn't do. "I know my Paul," I would say, "and he will far exceed their predictions. I pray that the doctors may see a miracle and be set on fire for the Lord." But other times I started to wonder how things would turn out. They warned me that Paul might not even remember me. I wondered who he would be when he woke up, if he would love me. I would feel the anger seep deeper into my soul. I wanted my man back. My heart ached for the sweet voice of my love.

☙ ❧

March sixth was Day Ten—a major medical milestone. "We made it this far!" the doctor gushed. It was difficult to know what to do with faith, how to distinguish between miracle and medical intervention. Paul's head injuries were so severe that at first the doctors told us that if he survived ten days, he'd probably make it. Later, as if by some cruel joke, they raised the number to fourteen because his secondary brain swelling was so severe. But I joined the doctor in celebrating—with prayers of thanksgiving and songs of praise—that he had reached this milestone.

Day Ten was also my father's birthday. He told me that the only gift he wanted was to see Paul sitting in bed smiling. Dad and Mom had taken turns staying at Paul's bedside. Though he already had one son, Dad was really looking forward to having a son-in-law. He recalled the summer vacation we'd shared at the lake, with its laughter and fun, the golf games, the hours of theological conversations, the hunting stories shared. He remembered the words his own father-in-law had said the day my parents got married. Asked if he was nervous, my grandfather had replied, "Yes! I'm expecting a son!" That's how Dad felt about Paul. He had already adopted him as a son and had only left his side long enough to make sure his other son, my brother, didn't miss too much school. The support my parents provided during this time was indicative of their faithful presence throughout my life.

☙ ❧

When I was little, I went to a nearby family friend to borrow a cup of sugar. It was just down the street and around the corner, but I had been emphatically warned to look both ways before I crossed the quiet road. Even so, my father felt compelled to follow me a short distance just in case. According to him, as I reached the road, there wasn't a car in sight. Nevertheless, I lingered on the curb, turning my head first left, then right, at least three times before moving onward across the street. The first time I ever learned this tidbit was as he shared it from the pulpit one Sunday morning as a guest pastor. Although the story was new to me, it didn't surprise me in the least. My dad has always been a gentle, yet constant presence in my life. He had a knack for understanding when I needed a firm hand and when I simply needed to venture out on my own, to gain confidence in my own judgment. When I was thirteen and returning home from boarding school, he took me on my first "daddy date." Having him listen to all my juvenile happenings made me feel important. But it was his interest in my thoughts and opinions that really allowed me to blossom.

Early one Wednesday morning during my first semester of college, I groggily answered the phone in my dorm room.

"Hey kiddo," came a familiar voice across the line.

"Dad?" I asked confused.

"Yeah, I was just calling to check up on you. I put a note to myself here on my office calendar, 'call Sarah at eight a.m. on Wednesdays.' I figure it's the only time when I know you'll be in your room."

This was the beginning of a sweet tradition between the two of us. Once a week, give or take, he would touch base. The calls normally lasted only about fifteen minutes, but it was enough. Sometimes we discussed grades, the health of my car, or the pressures of school.

Rarely anything really worries my dad or even riles him up, but the point of these phone calls wasn't to ensure my good behavior —he simply wanted to continue to be a part of my life. To this day, it's rare that a week goes by without some type of prearranged chat. During the tough times we consoled each other; when life got nasty I could always rely on his dry wit and realistic take on life. With frank skepticism, he was my biggest fan and my toughest critic. Whenever I had an idea, proposal, or wild adventure on the brain, I knew that my plan was solid and achievable when I finally got his nod of approval. He never wanted to get in my way, just make sure I knew what I was doing. But no matter how intense our conversations became, his heart was always the softest part I could rely on.

I guess you could say my father was the dreamer and my mother was the doer. Both were passionate, driven people but my mom was always the force behind us. Whenever we had a question, out came the encyclopedias. When we had a part in the school play, she was the master seamstress or acting coach. There wasn't a song she hadn't sung or an accent she couldn't master. Always laughing and pouring every bit of herself into those around her, our home was never dull. She grilled us before we went door to door in the neighborhood raising money for this or that school activity. Our sales presentation was important, she'd remind us as I walked out the door grumbling that it was only Girl Scout cookies. No adventure was too daunting or problem too large. Our first global escapade took the two of us to Monte Carlo, and since then we've been more than mother and daughter; we've been travel buddies and the closest friends.

Incredibly capable and professional, she is my Renaissance woman. She had several successful careers, each created around her family's schedule. Admittedly, she always wanted to be a mom, a fact that had always puzzled me slightly. Although she was a great mom, she was so much more than just a nurturer. Then one day it hit me; talented and ambitious, growing up in rural North Dakota, *her* mother had been the most powerful example of a person who could do it all. A farmer, teacher, hostess, politician, advocate, volunteer, musician; this woman could do everything, and the title of "Mom" was the only one broad enough to encompass it all.

As I grow older I realize what an incredible female legacy I have inherited, but the only way I think I will ever live up to it all is with her help. If tackling dreams were a love language, then it would be ours.

The intensive care nurses were the first to notice that Paul's ICP numbers seemed to stabilize and even begin to fall when more of us gathered in his room than were technically allowed. Paul had seemed more restful when we'd gather to pray or sing together; his heart rate and blood pressure would stabilize a bit. So they turned a blind eye to the groups that kept flocking into his room. It gave us all hope that maybe he was aware of our presence and that maybe thoughts were stirring under those swaddling bandages. And so we gathered and we loved amid the wires and tubes, finally closing each day with the good-night song the Olsons had sung to their children each night of their lives.

On Day Sixteen, Paul's ICP was stabilizing. He opened his right eye, but he was unable to see anything. The doctors informed us that the way he reacted to pain indicated he was in a deep coma. The deeper his coma, the more damage his brain had suffered. They used phrases like "permanently blind," "unable to speak or hear," "need to be fed through a stomach tube his whole life," "in need of constant professional care." I wondered if my faith was not strong enough, if things really would turn out that badly. But it was my second day with no tears.

☙ ❧

I'm crying now, though — months later in a doctor's office because of a panic attack. I look up at the doctor who is no longer holding her clipboard. "Strength is honed in trial," she says to me without rushing.

I nod. "Yes, but brute strength and sheer determination can get you only so far."

She agrees. "Yes, and that's why you're here. You need to find peace."

I know where that peace has to come from. Christ was strong in his suffering. He cried, he grieved, he was honest about his situation — but he did not complain. He did not find a way out of his situation; he accepted his vulnerability. He walked the valley of death and now we see the sweet rewards of his perseverance. Right now I'm not sure I would willingly go back and walk in this valley, but it's less scary today than it was yesterday. My situation is bound to get worse before it gets better, but it will get better.

"We are the most beautiful and strong when we allow ourselves to be vulnerable with God," my doctor says.

Yes, I will continue to trust him. *Please lead on*, *gently*.

Chapter 3

# BE THOU MY VISION

*Faith is deliberate confidence in the character of God*
*whose ways you may not understand at the time.*
Oswald Chambers

*P*urgatory. I don't believe in it theologically, but I do think I know what it would feel like if it existed. Dante had his Inferno, and I have my Limbo. At twenty-two, who isn't slightly out of sorts and perhaps a little naïve. Yet with all of my life experience, many days I feel like life is moving on around me, and I am waiting ... and waiting ... and waiting. Even worse, I'm not sure what I'm waiting for.

Eleven months after the accident, this should have been our first Christmas together, but here I am in my single bed, far from my broken beloved. Instead I drift off to a weary sleep in the middle of a deep prayer. In the world behind my eyelids, I find myself again on the ski hill that had been Paul's demise. This time we glide down effortlessly, without mishap. At the bottom of the hill that had caused so much pain, my memory ends and a new reality plays out before my eyes. Even in my dream, I know what was supposed to happen, and my heart still bears the scars of Paul's departure and my torment with the Lord.

My heart is suddenly in my throat and I throw my arms around his sturdy shoulders and laugh until I cry. I search the hills for others who had loved and lost Paul. And yet the world kept rolling, oblivious to the miracle that was in my arms. Unaware of what should have happened, friends from church tease and laugh without a care in the world. My elation is only mildly troubled by my lone recollection of what hadn't transpired on that fateful mountain. I had my love, and he had me. Paul, who was never afraid of strong affection, seems to bask in my abundant joy. I search his perfect face and eyes and breathe in his familiar scent.

Once or twice he prods me for the source of my exuberance. He laughs at my apparent silliness. But as he returns my gaze, he must see in my eyes the reflection of pain that had been lodged so deeply in my heart. I am as surprised as he that even in his arms I still feel the scars of suffering.

Without knowing what I'm looking for, I search the faces of all who had been such a comfort to me after the accident, all the memories of kindness and gentleness from those in our church who had taken such good care of us. Frustrated at my own ingratitude, I shake off the feelings and think about the future.

Time passes quickly before my eyes, but every detail is perfect, so extremely real—exactly as it had been those few months ago. The house I had shared with so many of my friends is just as we'd left it, our friendships and lives still intact. I run in to find my new world filled with hope and prosperity. All around are Christian women preparing for marriage and life beyond our cozy campus, without any knowledge of the accident or its accompanying sadness.

At first I watch with wonder at a life so still and peaceful, almost as if I am not among them. Paul watches me as well and attempts to draw me out. He wonders why I'm so quiet, so distant.

As he takes me in his arms, I realize there is a gulf between this world and me. All the people who loved us are different. The realization dawns on me slowly; they have been untouched by our pain. I am watching my friends as they *would* have been — carefree, without the tears and prayers and moments of tenderness that we had shared together, those moments that had deepened our love and granted us insight owned only through suffering.

Day after day flies through my mind. I see all the people who have been affected by our tragedy, and they are not the same people I know in my waking state. Life with them here is sweet and yet quietly empty. I don't care about all the minute details that used to matter so much — frivolous things like wedding planning and grades — and yet all the people in my dream still do. Hours turn into days and I find myself staring at others and searching for recognition.

I find solace and comfort in people I had never been drawn to before. I am still attuned to pain and find myself encouraging and comforting people I had never seen with my old eyes. Behind me was Paul, loving, stalwart, and true, trying to reach beyond my clouds and wondering where the girl he knew had gone.

I have an ache in my heart, wondering if anyone can touch it when I can't explain to them why it's there. Paul and my friends sense this ache, yet in the midst of their unscarred reality, they can do nothing to bridge the valley. Scenes come into view of friends walking through times of suffering and death, but the comfort I offer is unwelcome. My life seems too perfect; what could I know of their pain? I have not "earned" the right to speak to them, comfort them, or simply understand, as if I don't belong in their world or in my own. I understand their rationale. I had used it against my own "perfect" friends during my trial that they knew nothing of. Now in my perfect world I find myself longing to help, but I am barred from their circle. And somehow I feel alone again.

As my perfect life continues in my dream I am horrified by how unsettled I feel. How could I ever want anything more out of life than to have my Paul back? Maybe, just maybe, I ponder, if I can find someone who remembers — anyone who knows what sorrow we have been spared from ...

Lost in thought, we approach the door of the Olsons' home, Paul and I together, going home like old times, so sweet, so perfect, so untouched. I watch as siblings come running to the door to greet us with excitement, and we tumble into the house full of hugs and smiles. Suddenly Paul's mother pulls me into a strong, desperate embrace. Alarmed, I pull away and look into her eyes, and instantly it's all there. The sorrow, the heartache, the confused wonder of our suddenly upright lives. She knows! She understands!

Oh, what a relief — a strange burden, but what a relief! We weep, we laugh, and the words come pouring out over each other. We have both been radically altered in a world that kept on turning. We are the only ones who have been touched by Paul's tragedy, and yet in our perfect setting, it seems we are unfit for this ordinary bliss. It seems there is a price for this miracle.

In the absence of tragedy there is no denying how much Paul's life and loss radically affected so many lives. In my dream, my old friends haven't gained the deep understanding of life and the Lord's will because they were not tested, not tried. I see my own previous selfishness lived out over and over again in lives that didn't change because of the pain they hadn't suffered.

Time moves on and I seem to float as if on air, past the faces of those whose lives went untouched by Paul's suffering. As I realize their loss, I begin to weep.

🙠 🙢

I wake with a start, allowing my eyes to adjust to the darkness all around me. My hair is wet with tears that have flowed sideways down my face and onto my pillow. I dare not move. I want to live in this moment forever, between dream and dawn in my subconscious creation. As I breathe in the stillness, the memory of my dream rises again to my mind. It had been so lifelike and clear, none of the cloudy realities that haunted other dreams. Its vividness alone stuns me, but the realization that a miracle was planted in my mind for me, and me alone, is overwhelming. This wasn't just any dream; it was a gift, a vision of how God used Paul's life to touch so many, just like Paul had always wanted. Nothing would replace Paul or justify his pain, but the Lord gave me one more day with the man I loved.

Early morning light drifts through my window; the presence of God still lingers in my spirit, and I can't resist spending a little extra time with the Lord. Swinging my legs onto the floor, my toes grope for my reliable slippers as I head toward the kitchen to make my morning pot of coffee. After the pot begins to gurgle happily, I gather my Bible and mindlessly tap the button on the answering machine that I had somehow missed the night before. I am greeted by the familiar voice of the newly married Heidi Thornberg.

A startling blonde, she was always the calming, artistic side of our friendship. The two of us were comparable bookends of personality and looks, and we became devoted friends early in college.

In the middle of class two years earlier, Heidi had mentioned a strange phone call from an old contact asking her if she would be interested in being the liaison for Governor Lamar Alexander's wife, Honey. She may not have been initially excited about the concept, but I was and I guess my enthusiasm was contagious. Within a week, we were on a Greyhound headed to Des Moines, Iowa. We ended up taking the position together, and that summer we were a matched set of presidential campaign interns. When you find a friend who will cast their lot in with yours so completely, you have a friend for life. That summer I not only gained a friend but found myself adopted by a wonderful family. Years later it was her sister

I called after I was attacked, and she had looked after me. Heidi was the type of friend who always knew what to say in her gentle manner. Beautiful and talented, there was something about Heidi that made you feel lovely just by being in her presence.

Earlier in the summer, I had rushed to her side when she found out only weeks before her wedding that her father had cancer. Later, I walked down the aisle in a beautiful russet bridesmaid's dress and watched her father lift his daughter's veil. Again, I was amazed at how the Lord could give us such happiness mixed with such heartache. Heidi's father was one of the godliest men I knew, a counselor with an indomitable spirit, and it crushed me to see his thinning form. He had been a cheerleader to so many people so many times, and you would have thought he had handpicked each of our husbands by how much he cared for all of us.

Heidi's normally lilting voice is now strained with tension as it comes off my answering machine, asking me to come to the hospital as soon as possible. The family had been in the city for the holidays, and her father had suffered cardiac arrest. In minutes I am dressed and heading out the door, stopping only long enough to fill a travel mug with steaming coffee. I have an eerie sense of what the day will hold and know only too well how much emotional strength I can borrow from the strong cup of caffeine.

It has been many months since I've been in a hospital, since Paul's parents have moved him into their home, and yet I know it will be nearly impossible for me to summon the strength to go into that ICU. I pray with all my might that the Lord will guide me through the day.

Reaching the clustered family, I see Mr. Rapier's balding, cancer-ridden form lying silently in a coma, surrounded by loved ones. His coma is deep and unchanging. The sights and smells hit me with waves of nausea and I have to grab a nearby rail for support.

I try to move forward; gulping to fill my lungs with air, I will not be stopped.

Finding Heidi, I wrap my arms around her and sink into her family. At least I know this routine. I know the ebb and flow of conversation—some sideways laughter to ease the pain, beloved memories to share, and plenty of tissue. I know when to let this family sit in silence and when to offer a morsel of advice. I even know all the jargon falling from the lips of the doctors. All the scenes bring back so many memories, memories that can finally benefit someone. Arm in arm, Heidi and I walk through the hospital hallways.

"I want to show you something," I say moving toward the hospital chapel.

Although I've never been in this hospital I know it will be here. A quick glance around the small chapel, and I find it hanging on the wall as I had seen it before in another hospital. It had brought me so much peace, and I trusted in the perfect truth of the words.

*The Lord is my shepherd; I shall not want.*
*He makes me lie down in green pastures.*
*He leads me beside still waters.*
*He restores my soul.*
*He leads me in paths of righteousness for his name's sake.*
*Even though I walk through the valley of the shadow of*
*death,*
*I will fear no evil,*
*for you are with me;*
*your rod and your staff,*
*they comfort me.*
*You prepare a table before me*
*in the presence of my enemies;*
*you anoint my head with oil;*
*my cup overflows.*

*Surely goodness and mercy shall follow me*
*all the days of my life,*
*and I shall dwell in the house of the LORD*
*forever.*

Psalm 23 ESV

"Look Heidi, God never claimed that his children would not face evil or death. In fact, this chapter almost verifies their inevitability. But you know what I put my hope in? Right here, it's the strategic placing of "valley of the shadow of death." It's not at the end of the Psalm. No, instead, it's placed in the middle of this great testament to life with God. Death and suffering are not the final chapter or verse of our experience." Gently I reach out to touch the handstitched words, tracing the lines so lovingly created.

"See, death is tucked between two great promises. The Psalm begins with God's gentleness to nurture and discipline, promised in the first few verses. That's followed by testament to his unwavering presence and guiding strength in times of great pain. But the final words remind us that in the end, our cup will again overflow with goodness."

As if prophetically fulfilling the message of my dream, I am here because I understand their heartbreak. I can feel the hand of the Holy Spirit prompting, and I understand my purpose. Our lives have been woven together by a caring and tender God.

What amazes me is that I also receive comfort from them. Back in the hospital room, Russell's wife stands at the head of the bed and gently strokes his head. "You know," she says, smiling through the tears, "a friend of ours described his own coma as standing on a beach, knowing God was all around and being drenched with liquid love." I know that is where Paul is.

Just hours later, with tears streaming down our faces, we say good-bye to Russell. I smile, knowing that heaven is so much richer on this night because Russ is there. We leave the hospital at sunset. Eight hours have passed, and again I am absorbed into hospital time where life and death are all that matter; all the rest are just unimportant details. As I watch a shooting star fall to the earth, I feel as if a veil has been drawn back, and for a moment I am able to see the hand of God.

It's strange how emotions can fluctuate so drastically. As soon as I leave the hospital grounds, I feel a surge of anger, as if some dam has been broken. Heidi and her family have left the hospital, never needing to return. They know that their father is in heaven, and although it feels like the world they know is crashing down, they can say he is whole, once and for all. There is dignity in death. In the ceremonies to come, Russell will be remembered and honored. But what about Paul?

The words that passed between Heidi and me come flooding back: "In the end, our cup will again overflow with goodness."

〜 〜

One of the best gifts I've received was from a dear friend who sent me a cup, a very symbolic token of what the Lord was leading me through. My cup was emblazoned with many meaningful phrases of God's faithfulness and pictures of butterflies, a symbol that is spiritually significant to me.

This vessel is a tangible reminder that God has created us uniquely to glorify him in our own special way, through our talent and obedience in the midst of our experiences. Nothing is out of his sight or his power. But for this time, it is the Lord's will for suffering and for sanctification. My cup is a reminder that I am a vessel of the Lord's each day, in good times and bad. Each time I look at it, I remember I have a choice. I can choose to consider this time as a trial placed in my path to refine me. I choose to see it as an anointing of love even in the worst and most unexplainable of tragedies. I don't believe that God allows suffering simply to make us better Christians. Instead, I believe he has redeemed the brokenness of our world by using the suffering that breaks, to become something that makes us beautiful. He is not a God who justifies the means by the end. I don't believe that God sacrificed Paul's life simply to bring us closer to him. My God values every life with love and dignity; there is danger in our Christian tendency to try to understand God. On the contrary, when my cup overflows with tears, I stand in awe of the extreme measures God went to in order to restore us and offer an eternity free of pain, one of complete restoration.

> *During the days of Jesus' life on earth, he offered up prayers and petitions with fervent cries and tears to the one who could save him from death, and he was heard because of his reverent submission. Son though he was, he learned obedience from what he suffered.*

Hebrews 5:7–8

I know that my Savior experienced his own terrible betrayal and trusted that his Father would use it for the good of the whole world. Most days I find the peace to believe that my suffering is a sign the Lord has considered me worthy of his work. He chose to reveal himself to me with honor and love, even when his ways seem so far from my comprehension. My cup is my tangible invitation to participate in his world, in his ways, and then I realize what a miracle it is that this incomprehensible Creator cares enough to reside in me, a broken and simple vessel that is a pale comparison to him.

But tonight I feel like cursing my cup and my portion. Tonight there seems to be no rational reason, and all I am left with is the question of *why*.

*Going a little farther, he fell with his face to the ground and prayed, "My Father, if it is possible, may this cup be taken from me. Yet not as I will, but as you will."*

Matthew 26:39

Filled with anger and frustration, I drive back to Iowa—only days after saying good-bye to Russell. My purpose is to speak to a thousand people about God's faithfulness. I have no idea how I can do that in my current state of mind, but I have already committed myself. Earlier this fall, my father, a longtime elder of the church, had invited me to speak to his hurting congregation at my home church. Their pastor, a man who had been a rock for my family and me, was also suffering from cancer. The shock resonated through our church body as we all pleaded to God on his behalf.

"Hon," my father began, "this situation with Ray may not turn out the way we hope. Would you consider speaking to the congregation about what the Lord's been teaching you? I'm sure many people in this congregation could use a reminder of who God is, even if our prayers seem to go unanswered."

I wrestle with the question even as I drive to the place where I need to deliver the answer. What will I say? I don't have a happy ending to my story that will make it all worthwhile, no resounding theme that will make anyone feel good about themselves. But I do understand that God is still God, and that fact is enough for today. Perhaps I'm not the only one grappling to make sense of his will?

So when the moment arrives, I bravely stand beside my beloved pastor. Openly and honestly I share about Paul, our love, and what I am learning about loss. It isn't anything eloquent—my voice breaks every time I describe Paul's love—but no matter how angry I feel, I can't deny God's faithfulness.

In the third and final service, I take my seat and lift my eyes to the giant screen above and see Paul's smiling face. I hadn't realized it, but as I was speaking, they had been showing an array of pictures of a whole, kind, heroic, and loving Paul. My knees suddenly go weak beneath me as I realize this is Paul's moment. He is being honored and dignified right alongside the Lord today. The veil is lifted again. God knew I needed this communion service to honor Paul, even though I had discovered only days earlier that my heart ached for some way to eulogize him. A deep peace falls over my spirit again. As always, the Lord knew what I needed, even before I did.

My anger dissipates into a prayer of deep adoration. Not only has God given Paul the honor and dignity he deserves, but he's used my voice and my words. I couldn't heal Paul. Others much more skilled than I would care for him, and his home is rightfully with his family and not with me. But I have found something I can do for Paul, when all my other attempts seem to be in vain. I have honored him.

⌒ ⌒

Is purgatory simply waiting? Waiting for what? I suppose I'm waiting because I've given up any desire to hope. I am merely keeping a low profile, hoping that the "powers-that-be" will let me rest in peace.

"The LORD disciplines those he loves" (Proverbs 3:12). At first even this causes anguish because I have to ask myself what I have done to warrant this punishment. But with each step into faith, it becomes overwhelmingly clear that my Lord is introducing me to himself and his creation from an altogether different perspective. With each new tear I'm discovering the nuances of a Lord and Savior who has walked in my shoes and desires to introduce me to his reality. Discipline becomes synonymous with intense coaching and instruction. I am being trained for God's new perspective.

The more I struggle for God to fit into my former comfort zone, the more frustrated I feel. But by allowing him to strengthen my faith and increase my understanding, I'm seeing a completely new dimension of his life and love.

I have moments of clarity that reveal beautiful facets of God. For instance, Hebrews 4:15 says, "We do not have a high priest who is unable to empathize with our weaknesses, but we have one who has been tempted in every way, just as we are." I realize with gratefulness that we have an intimate relationship with a supernatural being who was betrayed and tried to the point of death. If anyone understands the bittersweet justice of our faith, it is Jesus Christ. There is so much hope in that alone.

I find myself looking at Christ with a new perspective. With awe I realize that a little baby came here defenseless and willingly, yet on some instinctive level he must have known what a broken place this was. Without glory or fanfare, he came here not only to conquer death but to experience it so he would be able to offer his nail-pierced hands in salvation and comfort.

Many people have been touched by Paul's life but even more have been touched by his pain, just like Christ. If I can communicate the power of God in his life to those who never even knew him, then I can continue to love Paul even if he can't love me in return. His love and his loss have shaped me, showing me who I am, what I am called to do, what my purpose is in life. I understand that my pain is never going to save me, it only gives me perspective and compassion. But if I can write from pain, then I can write from anywhere. To write is to love and to start to live again.

Chapter 4

# FEAR *of the* DARK

*Love is never lost. If not reciprocated,*
*it will flow back and soften and purify the heart.*
Washington Irving

They say that truth is stranger than fiction. Personally, I think truth can be just plain crazy. It means having your head and heart split in two every minute. Standing at the brink with your toes dangling over the edge. It's a place on my map where reality is broken and topsy-turvy. Wearing my insides on the outside, every step I take drives me further into the chaos. It's visiting the Olson home and wondering if I belong, it's sleeping in a bedroom covered in roses and ballet shoes. I lie awake on the bottom bunk in a precious room dedicated to young femininity, unable to fall asleep. The sweet innocence of his little sister's room is comforting and yet the childlike surroundings remind me that I have so much growing up to do.

I am on the verge of my twenty-third birthday. I feel very old deep in my bones, as if this past year has literally leeched the life out of me. But I have nothing to show for my weathered soul, and I slip off to my sleeping quarters as soon as it is appropriate. I lay in the dark listening to the laughing voices of the family telling stories, their sarcastic wit bouncing off one another. All six children, from two-year-old Piper to twenty-two-year-old Paul, easily chatted with their mother as if she were a big sister.

☞ ☜

Like some vicious circle, all the awkward emotions come back as if it was my very first visit. Back then, I cared so much about what Paul's family thought of me, and at the time it seemed the more I tried to perfectly fit into their world, the more awkward I felt. My family had trekked all over the world for the cause of Christ, and I had had powerful experiences with the Lord; but here where this preacher's family sat at the table and discussed theology and church happenings in their small town, my faith felt shaken. I'd never used words like "Arminian" or "Complementarian" in table conversation. I admit I didn't even know the meanings until later in my Christian education when a bespectacled professor shed some light on the matter. My family discusses politics and world affairs at the dinner table. My parents were pragmatists, and my father's drive for knowledge and justice spanned from avionics to geo-politics. They were advocates, advising missionaries and church leaders on a of myriad of issues. I had invested my young life into campaigning for causes, local and presidential issues that had seemed so important.

But in the Olsons' household I was lost and awed. A ministry veteran of Campus Crusade, now leading a thriving church-plant, Ken Olson represented everything holy that I wanted to be. Mary Olson held it all together with surprising wit. She wasn't exactly what I had expected from a pastor's wife, and her intense personality was refreshing.

The Olsons had been early campaigners of home school education, and Paul had graduated after twelve years under his parents' tutelage. Back in Wheaton, I had already met several people whose lives had been shaped by Ken and Mary's influence. These young families had Paul over to dinner just to glean parenting tips from him, a college senior.

Homeschooling, natural family planning, starting a new church, scrapbooking—all of their pursuits seemed more foreign to me than the Russian–Jewish children I had spent the summer with in Ukraine. But, oh, how my young heart longed to serve God; and this, this must have been the epitome of Christian living.

My mother had always warned me to be careful about whom I spent my time with. "You have an uncanny knack for molding yourself to whomever you're with, so choose wisely." The Olson household seemed like such an excellent place to be molded, but what if I didn't fit in? In my short life I had always been exotic, and deep inside I was afraid that I wasn't "Christian enough" for the Olsons, or for God. I had the distinct sense, like Donald Miller writes, that "If Christianity was a person, it wouldn't like me."[3] So I overcompensated. Growing up all over the world, you learn to blend in, and I vowed I'd do the same thing here.

In this family, men's and women's roles were clearly defined and everyone knew how they fit in. I longed to follow God with all my heart and to serve him faithfully, so I began to watch and soak in everything. If this was what it meant to be a godly woman, well, let's just say I threw myself into it wholeheartedly.

Of course, I had another motivation as well. His name was Paul. In what seemed like another lifetime, as another person, as a naïve and hopeful young girl, this home had become my sanctuary, this family my own. Had we been married, so much would have been different. But now sleeping in this sweet ballerina room will no longer be my privilege. The bridge to this life is broken.

---

3. Donald Miller, *Blue Like Jazz* (Nashville: Thomas Nelson, 2003), 47.

I should have been sitting on my husband's lap this weekend as I joked with his family, maybe even holding my belly in expectation. Yet I'm here in his little sister's bed. I thought I knew so much about life, but I have discovered a numbness in my soul. It's been building for months now, and at times it threatens to swallow me up. Before, it was only a minor side effect to suffering, but today it defines the better part of my existence. Like a butterfly that once flitted to the highest treetops, wind and weather have beat out any will to soar. Disappointment looms so near my door that I shrink back, unwilling to engage Paul. Now the butterfly stays among the wildflowers, eyes on the ground. It's safer there. Never again will I hope for things beyond my control; a dreamer's dream once bashed will fall dormant like the winter's ground.

I know where the numbness comes from, but I don't know what to do about it. Every time I approach the hospital bed and see the quiet form that once was so lively and loving, something in me dies. And yet no matter how hard I try to separate the silence from my heart, every time my fingers interlock with his and he refuses to let me go, my soul cries out, "No! He's here! He needs me!"

And then, mockingly, someone comments on how foolish I was to stick my fingers there. "You know he never lets go willingly," they say. "His grip is just a reflex." I stick my heart down even further into my shoes so no one will hear it breaking ... again.

But then again, who lets go willingly? Paul and I are the same. Regardless of anything else, we hold on to whatever is placed in our hands. We never go looking for it, and at times we are maddened by the thought of giving up, so we clench our fists and refuse to be mocked today. The solace of silence is sometimes the better demon than the reality of hope and loss.

Have I been gone too long and he's angry with me? Does he really need me, yet cannot communicate it? I know the man he was, and he was as gallant and loving as any young man could be, but any brave man can also be fearful of the dark, of being alone. And yet I cannot live in his world today.

I have no more to give. My insides have been scooped out and I am a hollow shell. Go ahead and demand love from me; ask me for feeling, desire, and hope. You may beg and plead, but nothing will you receive. You cannot squeeze blood from a stone or ask the battered butterfly to dance.

Long after the house has grown silent, I lie awake in his little sister's bed. He is downstairs in that infernal machine bed with the bars that make a person untouchable. But the overwhelming need to be near him overcomes my fear and all my common sense as I swing my feet onto the floor and pad down the stairs toward Paul's "special room."

I don't want to be seen. At this moment I wear my heart on my sleeve and can't handle anyone finding me neck deep in my vulnerability. But Paul is never alone, and this is the brutal truth of our life now. Slowly opening the door to his room I hear voices; the nurse that is staying with him tonight is reading to him, and instantly I am thankful for the gifted hands and attentive hearts that care for Paul round the clock.

"Oh, hi there." I have broken the reverie of the moment and the nurse stands to introduce himself. "You must be Sarah Kay. I've seen so many of the pictures, but it's nice to finally meet you."

Internally I wince at the word "finally." His intentions were sweet, but my absence has become obvious.

"How is he doing tonight?" I ask.

"He's having a good night. We've been reading *The Lord of the Rings*, haven't we, Paul?" As both of us look on at Paul, a heavy silence falls between us. I have stood here before, so many times, and it never gets any easier. I don't want to make small talk; I just want Paul tonight.

"Well, I'll let you two be alone. I'll just be around the corner if you need me."

Sensing my discomfort, the kind nurse moves into the office area, and I try to pretend there isn't a window between us, appreciating his sensitivity. I know there are cameras watching for his safety; I am all too aware that at any minute Paul will again need assistance, but for the moment we are alone. Leaning over, I kiss his cheek gently; Paul winces as if I had waked him from a deep sleep.

The right side of Paul's face is perfect, and if it wasn't for the medical paraphernalia, you would have no idea the seriousness of his injuries. Coming around to the left side of the hospital bed, I perch precariously on a stool and move the bars of the bed so I can be closer to him.

"Hi, Paul. It's me, Sarah," I whisper in his ear. I don't know if he knows who I am, but I reach for his hand to reassure myself. Paul squeezes my hand tightly, and I am suddenly choking back tears. Stroking his face, I am accosted with the smell of disinfectant and the whirring sound of machines slowly pumping food down a tube that winds down a pole and up under the sheets on his left side. My fingers linger on the scars that mar the handsome profile with Frankenstein-like cruelty. A deep unnatural dent replaces his left temple, pulling so tightly that his eyes seem sunken deep within his skull, twisting the handsome profile I love so much. But it's not these images that break my heart; it's the distance that sits between us no matter what I say. Tonight all I want to do is hold him. Hoisting myself onto the bed, I attempt to fold myself around his still form. I think my clumsy presence will annoy him, but I feel like it's the only thing I have to offer. How many nights have I tried to cuddle into one of those beds? Nights I have lain my soft form next to his, hoping that my presence would seep out of me and into his soul, into his quiet mind and stilled body.

As I lie there chattering mindlessly about college friends, books, family, the whole time I am trying to move something in my heart into a place that will allow me to tell him the truth. I am looking for a way to pour my heart out to him, some way that I could touch him, reach out to him.

I know what I can tell the man I love. Because he loved me, I can tell him everything. I can tell him how upset I am with him, how he has broken me. The longer I lie next to him, the closer I get to my worst fears coming true. What if one day all the words of love, kindness, and hope are used up? I worry that all that is left is pain and confessions. How can I give him such bitter seeds? Rationally I know that he hasn't responded to my words of love so it stands to reason that he wouldn't understand my frustration, but I can't risk it. How can I pour my bitterness out onto his undeserving body, especially when he can't fight back, can't disagree? What would he understand? What would he hear? I don't know what words will fall away and which will stick and grow. The awkward truth is that none of us really know how much Paul comprehends. Admittedly, in his presence I cautiously guard what I say, never wanting to be discouraging. The worst thought for me would be that during a moment of lucidity I would let my honesty slip and drop a bomb on his vulnerable soul. Hasn't he been through enough?

I do know the power of love. In life I had the power to wound him. But now so loosely tied to this earth, I want to take his pain away, not cause more. I could destroy him. Maybe I already have. What is worse, my silence or my confession?

As my mouth moves and my voice sounds chipper and sweet, I realize with a start why I have stayed away—like a ticking time bomb, I am sure that someday I will explode all over him and kill any part of him that is still there. I have never gotten through to him before. Why would I now? But my fear of hurting him, well, at least I know *that* is strong and I can hope it shows that I love him, have always loved him. Again I choose to protect him. I couldn't protect him when it mattered, when he needed me. Today I am forced to protect him from myself, to move on without him, and to be strong when he can't.

In the middle of my reverie I don't realize the nurse has approached, checking on the machinery that keeps Paul alive. I start awkwardly, feeling foolish that he has caught me curled around his patient, and I flail and flounder to remove myself from Paul's impersonal cage.

"I'm sorry, but it's time to move him. I waited as long as I could, but my replacement will be here soon and I need to make sure he's clean before he eats again."

And just like that I am dismissed. His health is more important than anything, and I leave the two of them so that Paul can have what little dignity he has left. Again I am thankful for the people that help him be a son, a brother, a fiancé. But I am not his caregiver, so what is left?

The heart is ignorant of medical terms, of twisted realties and self-made mysteries. Each day he moves farther and farther away from me. Each day I hope in vain. I sing and it's not heard. I scream and it falls deaf upon the stones. My worst nightmare is coming true. The man I love is being taken away from me. Paul is the only one who could bridge that chasm between him and me, between me and God, the giant space that spans between me and the Olsons, and he is somewhere else.

✿ ✿

Walking past the living room I notice I am not alone. Mary is curled up in her chair with a book, and I'm drawn to her comfort and strength.

"Can't sleep?" I ask, sitting down across from her and tucking my chilly feet beneath me.

"You know, it seems like I either can't sleep or I'm sleeping all the time." Her dry smile reminds me that we both seem to be observers of this thing called grief.

"How was Paul?" she asks and I struggle for an appropriate answer.

"Good," I claim with forced cheerfulness, and then the truth spills out like air from a balloon. "You know, the same, I guess." The honesty sounds pitiful on my lips. Mary puts down her journal and looks at me for a moment. "You know, he actually seems better when you're around, if that seems possible."

I smile and look away, touched by her honesty but unsure of my own thoughts. "Oh Sarah, I'm sorry. I don't mean to make you feel guilty; in fact, the more I get to know you, the more thankful I am Paul brought you into our lives. You know, I remember the first time he mentioned your name. You were a part of his big plan. Did you know that?" she says laughing, getting lost in the past. "He had to take the freshman music class, and he was required to attend all those concerts. He decided to make the most of it and began scouting for a date. I remember he kept talking about, what did you guys call it? Senior Panic?"

I smile knowingly. It still amazes me how close Paul and his mother were. He obviously held nothing back from her. Senior Panic is a common phrase among the like-minded young people of Wheaton. Although most of the students used it as a tired joke, we were all well aware that we had a limited amount of time to find our soul mate while surrounded by such a wealth of choices.

⁂

The memories of those early days came flooding back. Paul had been so perfect, so much an answer to prayer. Fresh off a short-term missions trip to the Ukraine, I had returned to Wheaton flush with the presence of the Holy Spirit. Taking a day to pray and fast, I had sought God for wisdom in the upcoming year, and I will never forget the peace that washed over me. I knew that my life would change soon, in the same way that God always spoke to me, like a silent voice. A junior and newly returned to Wheaton after a one-year hiatus, I wandered into senior level Rhetorical Criticism with a new major and uncharacteristic nervousness. This was a four-hundred level class; most of the students were seniors who were comfortable with their majors and with each other. As I stood at the door of the classroom in the basement of the Billy Graham Center, I must have surprised Paul, especially when I sat down next to the friendly looking senior with the warm smile.

"Hi! Is anyone sitting here?" I asked tentatively.

"Oh yeah. Have a seat," Paul offered, as he made space for me along the conference table.

"This *is* Rhetorical Criticism, isn't it?" I asked, slightly flustered after deciphering the maze of basement classrooms.

Paul laughed. "You're in the right place." I plunked my belongings down, and Paul kept talking. "So are you a grad student or something? I haven't seen you in a communications class before."

"Oh no, but it's a new part of my major. I'm an interdisciplinary studies major, a combination of three programs — communications, anthropology, and international relations," I chatted, as I pulled out my notebook.

"Oh, wow!" Paul replied, seemingly impressed. "Oh, and you're married?" he asked nonchalantly, as if he had just asked to borrow my pencil.

"Excuse me?" I asked, shocked and slightly confused.

"Married?" he replied casually. "My mother has a pearl wedding ring and your ring is on your left hand. Is that a wedding ring?"

I searched for some type of response to this very handsome senior. "Um, no ... I'm not married. This was a gift from my parents. It's my purity ring. That's why I wear it on my left hand. But, no, definitely not married." I'm sure I was blushing as an awkward silence passed between us. I was grateful the professor made an entrance and our attention was demanded at the front of the class.

I was proud of the pledge I had made with my parents to save myself for my future husband and had been a frequent peer speaker during high school on the subject of abstinence before marriage. But halfway through the lecture, I discretely switched the ring to my opposite hand. It was a very small movement, but it was enough. Without really thinking, I had confirmed Paul's hope. It was the beginning of something significant, and Paul walked out of class with a sly smile.

Over the next few weeks he began "bumping" into me in several places on our cozy campus. All this was a part of Paul's plan to land a date for the big concert in a few weeks. Before class one sunny September afternoon, I found myself on a park bench on the grassy lawn overlooking the Billy Graham Center. Casually Paul approached and sat down at the far end of the bench. I was taken by his easy manner and how tenderly he spoke of his faith. As the college clock tower bells rang out two o'clock, we carried our conversation down the sidewalk and into the bustling hallways. As we chatted, Paul asked me something about my faith and, as if with a sigh, something in me told me I could trust him. I was distracted by this pleasant feeling until I realized he had asked me to join him for dinner later in the week.

When the agreed upon day arrived, I sauntered into SAGA, the college commons, to find a lanky Paul propped up against the wall as if we had met like this a dozen times. We soon discovered that we were involved in the same church and had similar backgrounds and ambitions. Something lovable and intelligent about Paul had captured my full attention. I hardly ate any of my meal that night, so when Paul offered ice cream at the student center, aka "the Stupe," for dessert, I hungrily agreed.

As we walked out of the cafeteria, Paul admitted with chagrin that he had left his wallet back at his room. "Um, do you just want to wait here while I run back to my dorm and get it?" he asked flustered. "I live in Saint. It'll just take me a minute. Or I could meet you there. Or …"

Saint was so remote I had no idea how far it was, but I knew I enjoyed his company. "Or," I offered, "we could walk over there together. It's a nice night." As I said the words, a huge smile lit up his face. As we crossed the street, something I said made him laugh. It made me feel incredible. I made this intense, intelligent man laugh!

On the trip back we stopped at the great brick structure that was Williston Hall, the same dorm that had housed Elisabeth Elliot while she courted her husband Jim. Wheaton students had grown up with stories about how Jim Elliot, Nate Saint, and three other young missionaries had taken their wives to Ecuador to try to reach a cannibalistic tribe of Indians with the gospel, only to be martyred in 1957. In fact, two of Wheaton's dorms were named Saint and Elliot.

Paul stood in Williston's gracious lobby as I ran to get a sweater, undoubtedly unaware of how Elisabeth Elliot had developed much of her material on Christian dating for her classic book *Passion and Purity* while she'd lived in this very dorm. Seeing him waiting there so patiently in such contrast to the feminine surroundings seemed to foreshadow things to come. In a short while Paul would become a permanent fixture in my waiting room.

As we walked over to the Stupe, we discussed life and family. His easygoing and social nature pleased me. When we parted that night, I was floating. But it didn't help that none of my friends had ever heard the name Paul Olson.

The next night I had just returned to my room from a run when I was met in the hallway by a tall redhead who had been my friend since my first few weeks of school. "Hey, good-lookin'!" he sang out as he sauntered down the hallway. He popped his head in several open doors to say hello to friends.

Brandon was a resident assistant and a well-known and well-loved face on campus. Our freshman year, he had sat across a noisy classroom from me, casually spouting off one-liners. Tall and baby faced, Brandon was a homeschooler from Florida with a loaded personality. I thought he was the most obnoxious freshman I'd ever met, but our paths kept crossing. Soon we discovered we shared a long string of movie one-liners, and he came to fill the void that my little brother had left when I went to college.

Before I knew it, he was regularly sitting next to me in my Old Testament class, drawing puppet faces on his fingers and getting me in trouble. We went on only one date, an early Sadie Hawkins Day square dance, but because of him I was introduced to all my dearest friends. About a semester later we sat in a dimly lit hallway on the fourth floor of Blanchard Hall, having an RDT, otherwise known as a "Relationship Defining Talk," a common occurrence among Wheaties. If you've had a friendship or relationship with a member of the opposite sex, chances are you've stumbled into an RDT of some sort.

"Well, is it my imagination or have you been avoiding me?" I asked, frustrated.

Brandon hemmed and hawed. "See, SK," he started, using the nickname my friends had created, "it's sort of like this ... I haven't ever dated before and instead of pursuing you, I don't know, I just didn't know how to do it, so I guess you're right, I've just been avoiding you." He hardly lifted his eyes.

I sighed and laughed to myself. "Well, we've come a long way from when you thought I was a ditzy cheerleader!" I tried to break the tension. "But seriously, Brandon, sometimes you have friends in three categories: (a) casual friends, (b) people you grow to care deeply about but never actually date, and (c) someone special you want to spend the rest of your life with."

With that, we came to an understanding. We were *B* people.

Three years later, he had become a confident presence on campus and a confidant of mine, so I trusted him with an important question.

"B," I asked, "do you know a senior communications major by the name of Paul Olson?"

"Paul? Oh yeah! Great guy! That was fast, SK. How do you know him?"

"It wasn't that fast," I blushed and smiled. "But we did have a date last night."

"Really!" he smiled knowingly.

"Well, yeah, we went to SAGA, and then he took me out for ice cream." It was then that I realized this was Wheaton, and here, sometimes a date wasn't really a date. What could have been just an extension of friendship, I had turned into a date. I'd been away at a different school for my sophomore year and had forgotten Wheaton's unique dating rituals.

"Oh my gosh, B!" I gasped, mortified. "I didn't even offer to pay for the ice cream—I just assumed! I'm just used to a simple equation—going out equals date! B, I just walked right past the cashier! I don't even know if he's interested in me!" Brandon was laughing by now, but he always knew how to make me feel better.

"Sarah Kay, why wouldn't he be interested in you? But that's a classic! I'm proud of you. Always the lady. You deserve it."

I blushed, still embarrassed.

"You know what I deserve?" he piped up to take my mind off the subject. "A back rub." He grinned. To anyone else that would seem like a funny pickup line, but Brandon had always had the best intentions with me. "Please, SK? Honestly, I've been carrying fridges into dorms for three days straight. Plus if I ask someone at the dorm, with my luck one of the freshmen will think I'm flirting."

I rolled my eyes, remembering Wheaton's complicated dating scene with its many unwritten rules. Another rule of Wheaton dorm life was to keep your door open when you had mixed company during visiting hours. "Fine, but sit on the floor in front of me. And here, I'll show you my pictures of Europe."

I was trying to take the knots out of B's shoulders while he was oohing over the postcards from Krakow, Poland, when the half-shut door slid open and there stood Paul. I was sitting and pointing to some little detail, all wrapped up in Brandon, when in stunned silence I realized what this must look like to his unsuspecting eyes. In a heartbeat I pushed Brandon toward the door. All six feet six inches of him rolled across the floor as I jumped to my feet.

I stood rooted to the floor while all three of us exchanged awkward pleasantries and Brandon disappeared on some flimsy excuse.

I grappled to find something safe to converse about and reached for the easiest thing: music. I rushed to put in a CD. "Do you like jazz?" I asked. "I love jazz. Old jazz, new jazz, instrumental jazz, you name it. When I was a little girl, I could never fall asleep to the standard lullabies. I'd always lie awake wondering why someone would 'take my sunshine away' or why 'the cradle would fall.' My exhausted mother created a little song of her own, with a catchy tune and not many serious words. That tune was actually a jazz riff. Now when I hear jazz, it makes me feel dreamy, as if I am about to drift off to sleep, so peaceful." With a nervous laugh, I realized I was rambling on and on to this handsome visitor. Little did I know that jazz was what had started this whole thing in the first place.

Smiling, Paul spoke after what seemed like forever.

"Well, I just wanted to stop by to see what you're doing Friday night," he asked in his casual manner. Normally I would have been mortified to admit that I didn't have plans for a Friday night. But honestly, I'd been back on campus for a couple weeks now and was still trying to get reconnected to my overly responsible friends and their complicated schedules. Already I was getting sucked back into the "all work, no play" attitude that can prevail when you put too many type-A personalities in one place. I desperately needed a stress reliever, and so I admitted I was free as a bird.

"Well, good! I think a few of us are going to Chicago. A friend of ours is taking us to the Mexican Independence Day celebration in Grant Park."

Chicago and international culture? This was almost too good to be true. I had been craving an escape from our pristine suburban campus.

"I'd love to!" I gushed. What I didn't know was that later, while I was skipping around campus, Paul was begging all of his friends for the use of one of their cars, finally finding success. He wanted this to be special.

But I saw no sign of panic as I rounded the corner near his dorm and found him sitting on a bench in the courtyard. As it turned out, Paul's friends had taken an early train so it was just the two of us slated for the hour ride into the city.

This seemed a little daunting for a first date (or was it our second?), and I hoped we'd be able to fill the time. But as we talked, I was again impressed by how outspoken he was and found myself maxing out my limited theological knowledge to keep up as he made point after point on some subject raised earlier in class. As he asked me questions, I could feel my head spin. I had just come off an intense missions trip, but I was rue to admit that the finer points of my faith were very far from my mind. However, I felt more challenged than intimidated. And I was attracted to his intelligence. I knew I needed to marry someone that I had a deep respect for, and Paul's knowledge caught my attention. Here was someone I could learn from.

As the conversation switched to more frivolous topics, I discovered he was also a storyteller. The more I laughed at his self-described antics, the more colorful details he added, enjoying my laughter as much as I was. Time flew by.

Reaching Grant Park in a fit of giggles, we soon met up with Paul's friends. It was a chilly night, but the city swallowed up the four of us in its endless activity. I know we must have stuck out sorely, surrounded by local Mexicans in a celebratory mood. With my dark hair I looked like I belonged next to our tour guide, Janet (pronounced Yä net′), who was Mexican and had been raised in the city. But I didn't speak a word of Spanish. Neither did my African classmate. But that didn't stop him from buying all sorts of red, white, and green regalia; I guessed he was out to impress Janet.

Thankfully, we ran into Paul's Spanish professor who snuck us into where the real party was happening. Soon our friends were whirling around in a giant conga line, moving like a rhythmic snake across the crowd. I was in my element here and felt so alive. I noticed something in Paul hesitate, so without even thinking, I grabbed his arm and pulled him into the gyrating snake. Drastically different people, the two of us. I loved to roam the unknown, Paul loved to be boisterous in his own environment. I loved experience, Paul loved knowledge. It was like finding the other half of myself.

As we drove home, Paul casually mentioned the upcoming jazz concert, but by then I didn't need any convincing. Paul made me feel incredible and his offer was something I couldn't refuse.

After dropping off our friends, I thought our outing was finished, but Paul had one more stop to make. He needed to pick up some flowers for the girl who had so graciously lent us her car. I was again surprised as Paul began making a bouquet from scratch at the empty counter of the flower department in our local grocery store. It turned out that he and his buddies had made a point of befriending the local flower lady and were often there buying flowers from the friendly mother figure for all different reasons. Always quick to share his faith and reason for being, Paul chatted about several conversations he'd had with the flower lady as he casually packaged up a bouquet, complete with raffia bow. As he walked me home I held a single flower in my hand and a smile on my face.

"You know SK, I can tell that you have a really kind heart and a very beautiful spirit," Paul offered casually. It was the first compliment he had given me, and I was impressed that it was not about my appearance. The genuine observation went straight through me. I was hooked.

"You know, I think that's the nicest thing anyone has ever said to me," I admitted as I slipped my arm through his. And I meant it.

When the all-important jazz concert arrived, I came down those magical Williston steps to find Paul holding an amazing bouquet just for me. It was a beautiful night and neither of us wanted it to end. We found ourselves arm in arm, wandering around our cozy campus.

The more the night went on, the quieter Paul became. Something was clearly on his mind. Our conversation sputtered slightly, and it all came tumbling out as if he was afraid of my response.

"Sarah, I have had an incredible time getting to know you —you're fun and adventurous, smart, and incredibly beautiful." His honesty was making me blush, but I hadn't heard anything that worried me.

"My parents believe that finding someone to spend the rest of your life with isn't something you approach lightly, and so I really haven't dated before. I've been waiting until I was ready emotionally and spiritually to marry someone before I stepped into this arena. But now that I've met you, if you feel the same way, I would like to pursue you with marriage in mind. I hope that doesn't scare you?" he asked cautiously, looking down.

"I don't think either of us has anything to be afraid of," I replied, smiling. And a peace that passed over me gently wrapped its arms around us like the softly falling rain, reminding me of the stillness that had blanketed me in prayer only weeks before.

$$\sim \sim$$

The memory fades away and I realize Mary is watching me with gentleness in her eyes. "You know, Sarah," she says lovingly, "women are strong, stronger than we appear, but we need love. We need response. We need to know that we matter to those we love.

That is everything Paul can't do. I know that it was Paul's heart, soul, and mind that you loved and that he loved in you."

As she spoke, the unwanted tears escaped from my eyes and I chewed on my lip. Her tenderness was so powerful, and I found myself able to admit to her what I hadn't been able to admit to myself.

"His thoughts were my anchor and my delight. It was there that I fell in love with him, and we could have lived there for eternity. I feel like if it had been anything else, anything else that had been taken away from Paul, then maybe we could have had a fighting chance. It makes me so mad that his mind and soul were taken from me. I can hold his hand, kiss his cheek, and let the tears pour onto his face, but I can't penetrate the silence that surrounds him." Even as I speak the words I feel like I have betrayed him.

"On the good days I like to believe that he's communing with the Lord. For his sake, it makes me feel better. That's where his heart would want to be," his mother offers as if she understands me.

"And yet to think that they are communing together without me, well, it feels like they've turned their backs on me, like I've lost them both."

*"Amor vincit omnia,"* I mutter.

"What was that?" Mary asks distractedly.

"Love conquers all. It's Latin, and it's been bugging me for weeks. Don't get me wrong, I understand the Lord's unlimited ability to love, but I definitely doubt my own. In the darkest parts of my mind and my heart I'm terrified in my own limited ability to love. How strong is the power of love? For a year and a half I was loved more deeply than most women are loved in an entire lifetime. How can something that started out so beautiful become so horrifically painful? Can love really conquer all?"

"You know, when people ask me why God let this happen, I tell them maybe he was busy finding a parking space for someone." I can't help but smile at Mary's wry wit.

"But seriously, I don't know how God expects us to survive this. And then I try to imagine how you must feel. You and Paul were on the brink of your lives together, gradually removing yourselves from your parents' influence. But now, even as we try to stand behind you, it must feel so backwards. There isn't anything wrong with you or your love. And no matter what, I'm thankful that you've been a part of our lives."

Later I climb back into bed with a sleepy yawn. I don't know what we would do without our parents, and yet their assistance is a daily reminder that I am no longer Paul's other half or the one designated to make decisions for him. Gradually I'm turning over more and more of our life. Mary and Ken, Paul's parents, have grown in strength and wisdom each day as they gain more and more of an understanding of what's going on and the fact that their grown son is suddenly in such need of their support.

But this isn't how it's supposed to be. Skilled people take care of Paul from morning to night and what they can't do, his parents can. Nothing about our new relationship is natural, and no matter how loving and dear they are, I wonder if there's room in this life for me.

Tonight as the tears leak onto my pillow, I worry about waking up Piper. I sneak a peak at her and smile. I've known Piper since she was two years old. I had never met a man with so much devotion to his sibling, and she was an irresistible force in his life. We would rush home on weekends simply because he needed to see her. He realized how quickly she was growing up and didn't want to miss a second of it. I look at her asleep now, and I know that she has become my joy as well. It's rare that a tear is shed in the Olson household without Piper doing her famous little monkey dance to make you laugh. Yesterday I read her a picture book, and we both loved our time together. We used to play toddler games. In time she grew to love the ruby teddy bear I slept with and we would make up stories about him. The bear had been a gift from my brother, and in the lonely nights I needed something to comfort me. Recently though, I've found joy in telling Piper stories of her big brother and how much he loved her.

I know that in the morning Piper's sweet face will be next to mine, waiting (not so quietly) for me to wake up so we can cuddle or chatter. But I also wonder if that face next to me will ever be Paul's.

## Chapter 5

# BRING ON *the* RAIN

*Be still, sad heart! and cease repining;*
*Behind the clouds is the sun still shining;*
*Thy fate is the common fate of all,*
*Into each life some rain must fall.*
Longfellow, "The Rainy Day"

Wednesday morning, rain and peace wash over me with wonder. In days past, rain immediately translated into a long, bad day, as if my soul was weeping from the outside in. As the depths of pain would wash over me, I would start searching for signs of comfort and usually find myself alone and isolated. Being in the presence of deep pain is frightening. It's too messy; there are too many unanswered questions. "What do I say?" people ask, as if pain needs to be bandaged and plugged instead of released. And so they withdraw from sadness and grief. That, of course, leaves the hurting person alone with looming fear and sadness, forcing her to God for help. "Please God, fill me, heal me, nurture me. Do you really know how I feel? Can you really fill the gnawing pain that's ripping me apart?"

Today I see the rain with a newfound grace—grace that was hard-won through self-acceptance and time and a tender relationship with Christ. An uneasy restlessness has been stirring in my soul for the last few weeks. Perhaps it's the changing of the seasons. Spring has always made me think of new beginnings, new hope, a clean shiny slate. With the fresh air comes a rising doubt, a growing unsettledness that I can't place. Is it my job? My relationships? My spiritual life? Each of these is under a microscope, and yet I cannot seem to find any definitive answers. What is wrong with me? Over the last year, what have I achieved? Out of the rubble, what have I built?

Last evening I fell to my knees and lifted my eyes heavenward. Finally. It's the last place I've come to for answers even though I've known all along that it's the only place I should have gone. And it took a Hollywood movie to get me there. I watched *Signs* by M. Night Shyamalan, in which a pastor played by Mel Gibson is dealing with his wife's recent death. The poignant struggle of this bereaved husband to reconcile his loss with his understanding of God reminded me of my own struggle. I understood that his frustration and his denouncement of God were his own attempts to get back at him. Refusing to believe hurt him more than it hurt God, but it was the only thing he knew to do after such a horrible loss.

Something in me clicked into place, and I decided that I was not going to let my anger turn me against God. I didn't know how I would ever resolve the existence of both God's love and the world's cruelty, but I decided to let go of my need to understand. My fiancé was gone, but the Enemy wouldn't have my faith. So help me God!

As I sat before the throne of grace I prayed to my holy and very personal Father for guidance. As we sat there, I knew he was listening. My heart began to cry out — not, "God where are you?" but the more frightful, "God, where am I? How did I get here, and how do I find my way out?"

Deep in the recesses of my soul came an alarming answer, one that could be given only to one who is deeply loved. It was the type of answer that you get from someone who doesn't want to see you suffer and who is willing to tell you the truth, even to hold you while the truth sets in. In those silent moments the answer seemed so clear. "My child, I have never left your side. I can handle your anger, but to truly know me you need to learn to trust me."

It's an overwhelming thought. Could I really be angry with God? After all, he created emotions, all of them, so it stands to reason that the God of all creation isn't shocked by fears, doubts, and frustrations. Then I realized this Person knows what I have gone through, knows all of my mistakes and imperfections, and loves me. Just like that I began to cry.

I was able to hear this message not because of anything I had accomplished, but because of my utter desperation. Suffering taught me something.

Oswald Chambers writes, "We all know people who have been made much meaner and more irritable and more intolerable to live with by suffering: it is not right to say that all suffering perfects. It only perfects one type of person ... the one who accepts the call of God in Christ Jesus."[4]

Suffering is a concept we don't often hear about these days. It doesn't fit our modern mold for God—at least it didn't fit mine. My God answered prayers. My God took care of my problems. My God wanted the very best for his children. I had grown up in the shadow of stories of God's work. My family had taught me to pray with big expectations of God, and he seemed always to give us what we asked for. Using radio transmissions in Monte Carlo, my Christmas miracle in Swaziland, and the multiple occasions in

---

4. Oswald Chambers, *The Place of Help: God's Provision for Our Daily Needs* (Grand Rapids, Mich.: Discovery House, 1979).

the United States—this was my God, the God that could make everything okay in a moment.

But when does God ever fit a mold? Apparently only when he wants to. And the last few years of my life was not one of those times. I prayed, my family prayed, our church prayed, hundreds of people around the world prayed, and Paul was not miraculously healed. Still, I know God did not abandon us. He was faithful. There was so much I didn't know; my faith was so awkward, frustrated, and heartbreaking. The God I had relied on was gone, stripped away forever, but even in my blind groping, I could still feel something of him. A strange unnatural new growth was beginning.

I know that now. But at Paul's bedside and for the last year, I didn't know it. I couldn't understand. Paul and I were as shiny as a new penny. We had everything going for us on our spiritual résumé, and we were sure the Lord was going to use us to do amazing things for him. We had so many of the "right" qualifications, so why had God allowed this to happen? I felt like God was cut off from me, like my prayers kept bouncing off the heaven that had been sealed shut against me. Not only did I want my fiancé back, but the unanswered prayers caused me to feel weak before the people who supported Paul. They prayed and then asked me expectantly how Paul was doing. I had no good news to give, and that made me feel like some type of Christian failure. I had many nights where I was angry at God—nights I wailed against him, screamed, and carried on.

In the midst of all of that, he was so gentle. Like an old friend who lets you vent, he never passed on clichés or trite answers. It was as if he really understood what I was feeling.

⤚ ⤙

I need to take a long, hard look at all the clichés I have so often accepted. With my evangelical dialogue, it has been so easy for me to resolve the great suffering of others by saying something like, "But the good news is that three hundred people came to know Christ! Isn't that glorious?" As if the end makes the means insignificant. I don't have a wonderful justification for Paul's accident. All I have is tragedy, one man's gruesome, horrible pain.

But from God I have solace, friendship, and acceptance. With or without explanation, in Christ, I eventually find a place for my sadness. Sadness allows me to accept the emotional reality of tragedy and to own up to its consequences.

It's still raining, and I finally pull myself out of the cozy hole I had made in my single bed. Maybe I'll go run in the rain like I did as a child. Or maybe I'll just stand there with my arms outstretched and my face up, letting my tears fall to the ground with the rain, nurturing the earth and blanketing it in shrouds of quiet rejuvenation. I have a new freedom that I didn't have before, freedom in sadness that allows me to look into my soul and take ownership of my fragile state. I realize now that it is never wrong to be strongly affected by something or someone. This is a gift from God. I grab my jacket—but not my umbrella—and step out the door.

All of us were strongly affected by the loss of Paul. I love him, so many people love him. How could we not be affected? His absence marred so many lives, and it was never more evident than when his younger brother Peter married his high school sweetheart Amy. Amy's parents were Ken and Mary's best friends, and the entire community felt the loss even though it was a lovely occasion, a reason to smile after so much pain. I never once considered not going to the wedding, but I had never felt so alone as I drove into town.

"I know you didn't have to be here, but I am so thankful you are. I almost called you a thousand times to tell you that you didn't have to come." Greeting me at the door, Mary enveloped me in a long hug and tearfully tried to tell me she was glad to see me. I was confused—what do you mean I didn't have to come? Emotions were understandably running even higher than at a typical wedding and my presence seemed to calm some and frustrate others. I felt like a ghost, reminding some of their pain and of the past, while others were unnerved at my presence, as if they were guarding themselves against the day I would inevitably move on.

"I'm so proud of you for sticking with Paul, standing by him through all this," one woman told me as we chatted about plans to move Paul to a nearby rehab center. I was confused and muddled. Standing by him? It had been only six months! Of course I would stand by him. Not everyone agreed. "You are a beautiful girl. You should think about moving on." Move on? What were they talking about? Paul and I had a future. I couldn't fight the conflicting feelings and expectations; I seemed to keep sinking, but it was the actual ceremony that dealt the deciding blow.

"In sickness and in health, forsaking all others till death do us part." Paul's father led the couple in the solemn vows that mocked me with their simplicity. I never had a chance to swear my life to Paul. Even in this I was abandoned. I had no legal or moral right to any part of his life. I was on the outside and Paul was somewhere else, far away. I didn't know how I would ever survive saying goodbye. Paul lay silent, and at this time of new beginnings for his brother, something inside me died.

᷍ ᷍

I realize that our wedding bells have stopped ringing, and I also realize that I never committed my life to him. Whether I like it or not, he is not mine to hold on to.

My friend Emily was married the week after our graduation, three months after the accident. I didn't want to cast any sadness on that event, but as my own personal memorial to my love, I clipped my great aunt's antique locket to the trim of my bridesmaid's dress. Inside was a picture of Paul, taken on vacation with my family. I needed to take him with me.

Every part of the day was beautiful, and it was an honor to stand up for my dear friend. The wonderful thing about weddings is that they're celebrations of life, and I was in need of reasons to celebrate.

"Hey SK, want to dance?" a friendly voice asked. It was a simple question, but just like that I was exposed. I was still so new at being on my own that not having a date seemed like not having air to breathe. As Emily and Jeremy drove off in a flourish of bliss, my tender reality crumbled beneath me. The college life was over. People were moving on, and since I was staying in Chicago I couldn't help feeling left behind. My world was splintering into a million pieces, and I didn't know where I would land.

The only good news about Paul was the promise of transferring him to a Milwaukee rehabilitation facility specializing in head injury patients, Sacred Heart Catholic Hospital. Good news, but not exactly thrilling in comparison to a wedding. And things were happening out of my control, as if I were in a dream. His parents were his legal guardians, and I had little to say about Paul's life. His apartment was cleaned out and his stuff moved to his childhood home, decisions were made about where to place Paul, an exploratory trip to check out rehabilitation facilities was planned without me.

But the day they transferred Paul was the most joyful I had felt in months. We were moving on to a place that held so much hope, and I excitedly cleared out Paul's room to move to the next. We could leave this place of weakness behind. Nurses filled my head with stories of coma patients who had made good recoveries.

"And to think he had been without oxygen for over fourteen minutes!" an exuberant nurse exclaimed.

"He was?" I asked her, puzzled. "I don't remember that."

My mother was with me, and she smiled sadly. "Oh, honey, yes. You told me that right away. When you realized no one else in the family knew before the doctor talked with them, you didn't want to tell them; you must have forgotten."

I was stunned. I had so deeply buried something from myself, from his family and friends, that I had erased it from my memory. That should have told me something about my state of mind, but all I wanted to think about was my future. I moved into the adorable attic rooms of Paul's aunt and uncle, just blocks away from the rehabilitation center. Here I didn't have the distraction of school, and since we were farther from his parents' hometown, I was the only one who could keep vigil with Paul. It was finally something I could do.

The hospital was in an old section of town that had so much character for me to get lost in. Paul's room was just like any other hospital room, except it overlooked Lake Michigan and the view was incredible. Daily I would walk by the lake or stroll through the shops looking for books to read to Paul or ways to distract myself.

This was the first time I had ever had this much time alone. College was done and my entire life now was about healing and recovery. I was surprised how much recovery I still needed—I felt like I could sleep for days. I knew it was important to talk and read to Paul, but sometimes all I could do was try to squeeze myself into bed next to him, between the hard hospital bars and all the tubes, to hold him and watch TV. Other days I would wheel him into the hospital chapel. In Madison, the chapel had been very modern, with very few religious-looking images. The pagan-looking closet of a room was a stark comparison to this amazingly beautiful Catholic chapel with heavenly scenes of clouds and saints. We could sit in there for hours.

*We.* Plural. *It's him, not just his body,* I told myself. I was determined to have a future with him. I was still planning our wedding, a small affair. I had picked out several locations nearby that would work when he was strong enough, when he woke up.

"You know he's not in a coma anymore, right?" asked a friendly doctor during our first week at Sacred Heart.

"What do you mean?" I stammered incredulously. I had been imagining a scene in which he woke up to some level of restoration.

"With the depth of Paul's injuries, he has quietly moved out of a coma and into a coma-like state." I was devastated. Seeing the disappointment on my face, the doctor tried to give me some positive news.

"If Paul starts to respond well, he is welcome to stay at Sacred Heart for intense rehabilitation as long as needed."

But I was quickly becoming a realist. "What happens if he doesn't respond?" I asked, already feeling defeated.

"Well, Sarah Kay, we'll cross that bridge when we come to it, but failure to respond means he will have to be transferred to a nursing home or a facility that could take care of him until he could begin to benefit from their treatment and return."

It was too much truth to absorb, that any hope I had for Paul miraculously waking from his coma had evaporated in a moment. It was also the first time I'd heard the dreaded phrase "nursing home."

For as long as I could, I kept these words as far from my consciousness as possible. I walked the streets of Milwaukee and started planning, applying for jobs, looking for churches. I was thankful that this little nook of Milwaukee had so much personality. It played along with my delusion. In reality, Paul's condition worsened with seizures and leaking brain fluid, all requiring drastic surgeries and drugs, with the hope of a "response" fading into the background.

In Milwaukee the silence was deafening; my body sank under the pressure of watching a body that used to be so vibrant and loving deteriorate. The man I loved and respected was seemingly falling farther and farther away. How do you bridge a gap that seems to grow exponentially every day? I had very little of myself left to give, all I had left was Paul. I couldn't imagine anyone taking away anything else after I had lost so much.

A month later, in June, when I had returned to Chicago to be a bridesmaid at yet another wedding, I received the news that Paul would need to be moved to a nursing home. I couldn't breathe, I couldn't think, and all I could feel was defeat. Something in me broke once and for all. I had known the decision was imminent and yet, to take someone so young and exile him to such a facility was a death knell on any hope I had. It seemed the final diagnosis in something I just couldn't survive any longer.

Paul's new home disgusted me. All I could see was desolation, age, brokenness. How could this type of tragedy not affect us? . . . He loved me so much.

≋ ≋

"Hey, Sarah Kay," a classmate had called out during my junior year at Wheaton as he sat down next to me with an inquiring look on his face. "Were you in the cafeteria yesterday around two o'clock?"

It was an odd question, but I answered as honestly as I could. "No, I have lunch at twelve thirty. Why do you ask?"

"Well, some guy climbed up on the stone fireplace with a megaphone and yelled out to everyone that he was madly in love with a girl named Sarah Kay."

My heart stopped and another voice behind him chimed in. "Yeah, I heard that too. Except I was studying at the Stupe. The guy climbed up on the table. Another guy was with him. They had a video camera."

My face must have turned the color of cranberries because I was now the center of attention, and they quickly figured out that I had no idea what they were talking about.

But I definitely knew who was to blame!

They all smiled at my confusion. Wheaton was not exactly a place that supported releasing your inhibitions. Even most public displays of affection were watched warily — unless of course it was a giant engagement ring, and those popped up each spring by the bushel. This new endeavor, however, was most unheard of, and I shook my head in amazement. The crowd around me dispersed as I slunk out of the class, I but caught the murmurings as people discussed the oddity. "Well, I know it had to be you," someone said with a shrug. "I don't think I know anyone else who has the name Sarah Kay." I suddenly wished I had a name like Jenny or Emily.

Still crimson, I moved on to my next classroom and was surprised to hear my old Bible study leader call out to me. She ran at me and breathlessly said, "Sarah Kay, I heard someone with a megaphone — "

"I know, I know. At the cafeteria. I heard ..." I said, rolling my eyes. She looked at me confused.

"No, not at the cafeteria. There was a guy with a camera and some other guy had climbed onto the roof of Williston Hall. He had a megaphone and everything! Are you engaged or something?" she asked excitedly.

"No! I've been dating him since August. This is only January!" As I walked away from the conversation, I resolutely picked up my books and headed out of the classroom. I could not sit through another class like this. I had to figure out what was going on.

I was terrified that Paul was going to propose. Not that I didn't want him to—I just didn't know if I was ready. Paul was nowhere to be found and my roommates acted as close-mouthed as cats with canary feathers lodged in their whiskers. I knew my birthday was coming up, and so I did the only logical thing ... I prayed. Terrified and emotional, I made a foolish pact with God.

"Dear Lord, I just need a warning. Help me prepare my spirit. If Paul is going to propose, give me sunshine that day. If he's not, please make it rain."

The day of my birthday dawned with gray, grimy weather, and I found a shiver of excitement. I had never been so glad to see that cold gray rain, and I went about my business with a skip in my step. I didn't find Paul before chapel where we usually met—and Paul was as predictable as a watch—but I was caught up in a throng of friends so I didn't worry about it too much. I walked out afterward and there he sat holding a single rose. I smiled, full of warmth—the sentiment was nice and mellow, fitting with the foggy weather. As he walked me to my class, we walked past a car, and I was completely taken aback as he opened the door to this strange vehicle—until I saw the dozen or so roses sitting on the front seat and the impish grin on his face.

"My lady," he smiled.

"What is this?" I stammered as I crawled inside and my friends waved at me with devilish grins.

"Well, I called your teachers and they were more than glad to excuse you today."

It turned out that Paul knew I had a favorite restaurant in Chicago, but the only reference he had to it was a black-and-white picture of a group of us taken in the wee hours of the morning after a formal a few years back, a little diner in a Chicago neighborhood that I had stumbled upon while exploring the city years earlier. In order to keep it a surprise, he'd spent hours on the internet tracking it down, rather than asking one of my friends the name of it and risk them spilling the beans to me. The car swooshed us away to a cozy brunch there, and then we spent the rest of the rainy day in Chicago, in museums and coffee shops, just reveling in each other's company.

It wasn't until we returned to Wheaton and Paul made us stop in the lounge to pick something up that I got nervous. It was the end of the perfect rainy day, but Paul had something up his sleeve and was notorious for crazy antics. Living up to his reputation, he popped a video into the communal TV, and soon I was watching Paul all around the city declaring his love for me. Either with a megaphone or sitting on a street corner with a sign, he had put together the craziest montage I had ever seen. It all made sense now, and I was able to enjoy his creativity in spite of how mortified I was.

After that he swept me away to a restaurant full of all my friends who had gathered to wish me a happy birthday. The question burning on everyone's mind was if I would walk through that door with a ring on my finger. I was thankful that Paul would go to all this work for my birthday, not even needing any other excuse to go all out. It was one of the most special days of my life.

⌇ ⌇

I look up from my frolic in today's rain and catch a glimpse of a neighbor looking out the window, apparently confused by my antics. I laugh and turn back toward my door. Time for a hot chocolate. I can't stop at sadness. I have to appreciate not just my loss, but also the abundance in my life.

Wheaton is not a perfect place, but I can't imagine a better place to be when your world crashes down. Within days of the accident, Paul's photo was plastered all over the campus. Classrooms held regular prayer vigils and daily prayers were spoken from the chapel podium. The majority of my professors were saints (the others were an introduction to the hard reality that was to come).

The day I walked across the Wheaton graduation stage was like a dream. My parents and Paul's parents were there. We all looked weather-beaten, but thankful. John Piper, one of Paul's heroes, gave the commencement address, and as I walked across the wooden platform, I thanked him for the foundation he had helped lay in our family's faith. All day I had been chewing the spot on my lip that kept me from crying, and this consumed my focus as I walked toward the stack of diplomas. Suddenly the entire student body was standing on its feet. President Litfin's mouth was moving, but I only caught a few words over the noise and my surprise.

"So sorry for your loss ... in our prayers ... very proud of you."

The highlight of my day was being in the arms of my dearest friends. In the days after the accident I had an incredible support team. Almost immediately, Elisa, Emily, and Annika were at my side, and at graduation time I found myself sitting at a table, surrounded by love and strength. On each side, framed in perfect symmetry, sat a beautiful, tender, and unique woman — three brunettes and one sporty blonde, all different and yet all gracious and intelligent. As I sat in the restaurant across from the hospital, I realized that the forces had assembled, and for a brief moment my world felt balanced. The four of us strange compilations of females completed each other like four legs of a table.

An unspoken chord had been struck when we met, and a quartet was made complete. It had been decided in college, late December of our freshman year when allegiances are still fledgling, and quickly we had become a force of femininity. The accident was unlike anything we had faced in the past. But we were in it together. In the midst of their own senior finals, job interviews, and wedding planning, it was a miracle that at least one of them was with me at nearly all times—guiding me, steadying me, communicating for me, shielding me, whatever it took. What would I have done without these marvelous friends who nearly carried me through the ordeal?

Elisa—the oldest and most petite—is an intellectual power who is slow to speak and yet always decisive. A gorgeous intellectual, I nicknamed her "Muscles" because of the way she could use grace and charm to get us to move through problems. Audrey Hepburn wouldn't hold a candle to her delicate warmth, and yet she has become the quiet force that I have leaned on over the years. Few people have I found so comfortable and so inspiring.

As heaven would see fit, Elisa's polar opposite was, of course, her freshman roommate, Emily. A fiery Midwest gymnast, Emily is spunky, beautiful, and always full of energy. She is so full of life that when storm clouds pass over her, everyone feels the chill. And yet so engaging is her personality that when it's time to play, few can resist her devices. But under all her competency is a woman who is deeply committed to hearing the Lord's still small voice. The first time Emily came to my door with a problem, I was deeply touched. To think someone this well-liked and fun loving could ever need my advice surprised me. But then again, she's always tapped the most dramatic sides of my personality.

And then there is my other steadying factor, Annika—beautiful, talented, wholesome Annika. She had wanted to be a first-grade teacher since the day I met her. Capable of all types of silliness, Annika takes you by surprise with the stillness and depth in her eyes. She is the one people would go to when in need of a listening ear. She sends kind notes and thinks to ask others how they are doing. Raised by artistic eclectic parents, she had the best sense of who she was and encouraged me to be true to myself.

Some days I wondered what I could contribute to such an amazing group of women.

"You know you're the glue that holds all of us together, don't you?" Annika told me one day while we were in the hospital. "I was thinking about you on the way up here and you've always struck me as the most people-oriented person, the one to drop everything when one of us needed to talk. We're all definitely type-A personalities, worrying about shoulds and need-tos, but we always needed you to tell us when it was necessary to prioritize and have girl time. You've always had the strength to carry our burdens as well as your own, and you were able to sense more than anyone when we all needed a breather. You would force us, in a good way, to really seek one another and connect, often saving us from our short tempers and sensitive spirits." As Annika stroked my hair, I felt at home. It felt so good to be understood.

The best thing about being a part of this circle was that we knew we belonged to each other. I have many beautiful friends who have touched my world deeply, but this was more than a simple give-and-take between kindred spirits. The four of us, well, we were a matched set. Each of us think and speak and worship and encourage and work in dramatically different ways, but we all agree that the Lord is our God—and that *Steel Magnolias* is one of the best movies ever made.

We had gathered in joyful giggling times and in deep heartfelt moments in the past. But on graduation day, as they encouraged and clucked gentle words, we all knew quietly that things would never be the same outside the safety of our foursome.

Some of my safest memories are of those beautiful women swooping in and pouring out love and laughter onto my bitter, aching soul. Across the table someone would remind me that I was so strong and that they were so thankful for me and my spirit. But most nights, when strength seemed far from reason, it was simply important to belong.

And my family, of course, stuck by me. My parents came whenever they could, and so did my little brother. He was such a trouper. Dana, a tall, talented senior in high school should have been living high on life. Instead he was playing with Piper, the littlest Olson, trying to distract her from the sadness all around.

Siblings make wonderful sidekicks. Dana is four years my junior—just young enough that I could boss him around, but old enough to be my playmate.

As kids we woke one morning in Kenya to hear a large something trotting along the roof. Always far too curious for our own good, Dana and I headed out to investigate. I had all the eager fortitude of a young Dr. Livingston going out to conquer this strange beast, while my six-year-old brother brought up the rear with a handful of crackers stuffed inside his mouth, the other hand grasping the box for good measure. As our pajama-clad search party rounded the corner of our city dwelling, we ran headfirst into a very large, very hungry monkey.

The advantage may have been to the monkey because it was seated on top of our family compost heap, but I don't think I would exaggerate to say it was the size of an average kitchen chair. An impressive sight to begin with, it made itself even more frightening when it opened its mouth in a screech, showing off an unruly set of incisors that could have bitten off the hand of a small child, at least according to my reliable imagination at the time.

In a moment of panic, Dana and I shrieked back at him and sprinted for safety behind a large tree next to our house. It wasn't until we turned around that I realized Dana had shed the box of crackers in our retreat.

"Dana! The crackers!" I cried, realizing we had left our prize undefended. Being young and obedient, he rushed forward without any hesitation at my command to rescue the crackers from the terrible beast.

The beast took quite an interest in our forgotten booty and began to amble its way off the trash pile and toward the crackers on all fours, just as my little brother charged. In horror, I watched the monkey stride toward the cast-off crackers, just as towheaded Dana in his yellow pajamas burst from behind the tree to sacrifice himself for his sister's wishes. Head to head they moved, these strangely matched foes.

The young boy proved to be the more ambitious of the two and returned to my side, jubilant in his conquest, presenting the box of goodies as if it was the Holy Grail. In a moment I smiled at him and this amazing show of devotion, then with a flood of emotion I cried, "Don't you ever do that to me again!"

Thankfully we both grew up, only Dana now has the advantage over me and towers above his "big sister" by nearly a foot. For all the stories we have and experiences we shared, including discovering Froot Loops and sleds on our return to the States, we have been the best of friends. We also learned to relate in a series of movie quotes and punch lines that became our secret code. The goal was to make the other laugh, and to ourselves we were comic geniuses. My dad called it Twin Speak, and it continues to get us in trouble to this day.

In time we discovered that although situations or relationships would change, we would always have each other. Dana is a man of unwavering character with a tender heart. Always a thinker on deep levels, humor became a quick and easy way for me to understand him. I don't know who I would have been if I didn't have his unchanging devotion. "I don't know how you do it," he said to me one day. "You seem to walk into any situation and figure out a way to be successful. You also break every conventional rule to get you there." Like reading a fortune cookie, my little brother had summed up my life in a sentence.

In addition to being sidekicks, siblings are also extra parents, to complain to or to defend. Dana was the kind observer to my life, rarely advising but always there, comprehending better than anyone else. That's what hurt so badly about the accident; I couldn't protect him from it. His life was affected by my tragedy, but he was never bitter. He is one of the most inspiring souls I have ever met. With both of us out of school, he would come and spend time with me, quietly willing me his strength. I so needed it and was thankful for the company.

My company now—as I sip my hot chocolate and listen to the rain—is the gentle presence of the Holy Spirit, and it's not something I take lightly. My story is not over yet.

Chapter 6

# AN ALABASTER JAR

*The knowledge that makes us cherish innocence*
*makes innocence unattainable.*
Irving Howe

Some days I wish that every department store was like Nord-strom Rack. I wish having one huge communal dressing room with big mirrors and lights was mandatory by law. The best part about it is that no matter what shape or color or income, every woman that strips down has something she wants to hide when she's standing in her underwear. In that dressing room we are all exposed. One has a flat chest, the other big thighs, and on and on. Soon you realize there isn't much to feel bad about.

I've been out of college for a year now; I always figured I'd have life figured out by now, but it's tough to be a woman in the twenty-first century. So many images flood my consciousness on a daily basis, all telling me who I should be and what I should look like. In the deafening roar, how will I know who Christ wants me to be?

Ever since I was a sophomore in high school I've struggled with the demons of perfectionism and self-image. As I let the Evil One fill my mind with lies, I sank deeper and deeper into destructive behavior.

To quench my raging insecurities, I reached out to food to insulate my heart. Then when the guilt of what I'd done would surface, instead of turning to my Lord in remorse, I would take the end of a toothbrush and stick it down my throat to vomit up my guilt. Sometimes I would purge my silent obsession over the kitchen sink in an empty house, sometimes in the basement bathroom in the dark of night.

It always started with a nagging doubt that other people were having more fun than I was, or that I was falling short in some way. If only I could be perfect, then I would be lovable. If I could just lose a few pounds, everything would be okay. I would be okay. Then I would be accepted. Then I would be loved. Then I wouldn't have to worry about rejection or anything else for that matter.

But the ache would grow and I would do anything to stop it, including inhaling anything edible in my path. I was a "dysfunctional dieter" and a bulimic, and my need to be perfect was eating me from the inside out. Diet drinks, diet pills, cabbage diets, starvation diets—you name it, I tried it. It didn't help that most of the food I ate had so few calories. I would end up devouring food in the afternoon to quench the hunger and create a numbness of escape. I had been starving myself for perfection, craving love and approval. When I finally caved and filled up my stomach, a dull warmth would consume me, never quenching the ache, just smothering it. As I cooperated with the obsession, the lies sank deeper and deeper into my heart. Mood swings, neurosis, it was all embedding itself deeper into my spirit as I sold my soul for a smaller pair of jeans. Soon I wasn't enjoying the fellowship of eating with others, and my lovely singing voice was strained and raspy. I was driving myself further from my friends and family and closer to destruction. Anger and unspoken frustration raged through my veins and I grew harder to live with. I had set such unreal expectations for myself that no one could reach me.

One evening, on a spring choir tour in Orlando during my junior year of high school, I had left my bikini-clad peers and sought refuge in a quiet hotel bathroom. With my head on a chilly toilet seat, my heart wept. "Lord," I whispered, spent and weary from forcing my body and emotions to undergo such a terrible secret, "I don't want to live like this anymore."

As I sat there quietly, a veil was lifted from my eyes and heart. I got up, washed my face, and went hunting for a bottle of water. Wandering into the warm Florida night, I drank deep breaths of air. Everything seemed to sparkle, and I had never felt so clean or free. The rest of the trip was a dream, but it wasn't until we returned home that I had proof it hadn't just been in my head.

"You know, you have always been beautiful," a classmate remarked, casually flipping through photos from Florida. "But on that trip you absolutely glowed." I have never forgotten her simple statement or the power of God's beauty.

Since that day, my desire to purge practically disappeared. My thinking still needed to be reorganized along healthier lines—I had spent too many years running from God's peace and running to food, so the journey into a place that was "healthy" was a long one. Even now I have to check myself to ensure I don't go back to unhealthy thinking—but I was strengthened by good counseling and amazing friends and family.

Knowing that God understood my agony and cared about me and my secret desires was such a tender relief. My bathroom moment was a giant step for my seventeen-year-old soul, and the Lord honored my stifled prayer. I'll never forget the freedom and peace that washed over my tired frame.

John Piper attests that our happiness and God's glory are not separate realities for the Christian. They are the same—the goal and the aspiration. This has been a revelation for me, as well as a relief. My changing attitude comes from him, and the wearying fight between my destructive desires and his will is not for me to overcome by myself. Instead, from him comes a grace to change and grow. Perfection is not for me to attain, but his grace to live and love is lavishly poured down upon me.

⤞ ⤝

The people-pleasing tendency is hard to break though. I had it even as an adult. Days before Paul's accident, a small band of concerned friends sat me down and began gently probing into our relationship. They all loved Paul, but for this moment they wanted to focus only on me.

"Sarah Kay," Emily began, "we've been praying that Paul is the right man for you."

"We hope that he is," Brandon quickly inserted.

"Yes, that's true," Annika affirmed. "But our main concern is that you're trying too hard to become the person Paul wants you to be. We want you—no, God wants you—to be true to yourself as you grow in your relationship with Paul."

I might have started off a bit defensive in my response to them, but the Holy Spirit was present and I could sense nothing but kindness and love in their words. They promised to support any decision I made and to prayerfully walk beside me.

"Just keep asking the right questions," Elisa counseled.

A door opened in my soul and I felt relieved. I'd been struggling silently with the Lord. I had been forcing myself to become everything I thought God wanted me to be, but some days I wondered if I was conforming to God or to Paul. This question had been sitting heavy on my soul. It seemed the more I tried, the harder it became. I had cried out, exhausted with the need to please Paul—and God—but dutifully moved forward, not knowing any other way.

I honestly poured out my fears with Paul, even confiding in him all the comments of my worried but loving friends. I told him that if the peers we both respected had concerns, we should honor that and again place our relationship before God. Paul's peaceful understanding and support confirmed to me that this was God's leading. The grip of fear and perfectionism loosened, and I took a refreshing and holy breath. I wasn't sure how we would move forward, but for now it was simply enough to acknowledge the question.

"Sarah," he offered cautiously, "I've grown up with strong ideas of what my future would look like. Some of that came from my background, but I think most of it is the result of my own expectations. I also realize that it may seem overwhelming, but that's my fault. I realize how brilliant you are, and sometimes it doesn't seem like you fit into my world. But you're even better than anything I could ever hope for. If you can't be true to who God created you to be because you're trying to please me, then yes, something is wrong. And I will admit my ideas get in the way, but we both need to be honest and face this one day at a time. I've learned so much from you, and I would hate myself if I didn't get to spend every day with you." Paul's words went straight to my heart and it was a powerful lesson for both of us. I realized how important it was that I be completely committed to being the woman God had created me to be and nothing else.

～～

Sadly, three days later none of it mattered as Paul lay helpless in the snow. In that moment our lives had been ripped apart. Here I stood whole and anguished, and Paul lay broken and silent. My commitment to him renewed when I saw that he needed me, and I cried out desperately to the Lord to unite us finally in health and hope.

Only later, as survival seemed to push us farther apart, did I begin to wonder again if we were really meant to be. When Paul was weak and I was forced to be strong, the Lord met me, and the tragedy stripped away any pretense. Somehow in the middle of all the wreckage, I was finding my voice. Why did it have to happen now, in Paul's absence?

☙ ❧

The night of Paul's and my first kiss, the gypsy in me made a prediction. I warned him that if he stayed with me, I would introduce him to all that he had been sheltered from—life outside the box—and he would be my solid ground, my unchanging stalwart. I just didn't know how soon this prediction would come true.

For Paul, truth was crucial; for me compassion was. This was often a source of frustration for the two of us; what I saw as living life to the fullest, Paul saw as rebellious. Sometimes it was the little things that brought out this difference.

☙ ❧

"Did you ever just need to get away?" I asked him in passing one day.

He didn't know what I meant.

"In high school, if life was just too busy and I wasn't ready to come home, I would just drive. I'd drive right past my house and into the rolling Iowa countryside. It was gorgeous and I would have the most amazing prayer times with the Lord, just driving, thinking, praying."

"You would just drive?"

Smiling, I reminisced like it was yesterday. "Yes. One time I couldn't find my way home, and I had to stop at a pay phone in front of the courthouse of the next county. I called home and asked my mom, 'Where is Anamosa and how do I get home from it?' My mother thought it was hilarious," I chuckled to myself—until I saw the look on Paul's face, a mix of shock and dismay that stunned me. "What?" I asked confused.

"My parents would have killed me if I hadn't come straight home!"

I felt like I'd done something wrong. I didn't know what to think. "My parents were very strict about the important things, but they allowed me the freedom to explore," I told him.

"Did you tell them you'd be late?"

I didn't answer the stated question, but I did address the implied question. "Paul, I know I'm far from perfect, but this is not one of those things I need to be ashamed of. I've always worked hard to live a pure life, one God and my parents could be proud of." I was thinking about some of the people I have mingled with who couldn't say the same thing, but I didn't mention that to Paul. He wouldn't understand how getting to know them had helped me in my commitment to God.

Often with Paul I felt like I had something to hide. Purity for Paul and me had been a double-edged sword. He introduced me to the black-and-white of truth and concept, and I drew him into the messy gray of life outside of theory.

One summer night in an idyllic setting, our differences came out with frightening clarity. The sun sank low over the lake in a beautiful, lush glow. Somewhere a loon sang and the frogs echoed their response. I sat curled with my head on his shoulder and put my legs in his lap. We had not had time together like this in ages. The past few days had been beautiful, probably because we both knew we were going to make a life together and were enjoying that security. This time was supposed to be spent with my family, but our longing to connect drove us into solitude. My family had gone to bed, and neither of us was disappointed.

Paul sighed with contentment.

*How can he be content?* The thought flitted up from somewhere deep in my soul. I tried to stop it but couldn't help scoffing at his naïveté. How could he be so blissfully happy? Isn't there more to love than this? His deep affection washed over me time and time again. And yet ... what? The question hung like the sun over the rippling water—so present, yet so far away.

He pulled me closer.

Paul had never kissed anyone before me, but I had kissed a lot of frogs.

"You're beautiful," he whispered, our faces close.

I saw something in his face. Was it desire?

"I love you, Sarah Kay," he breathed deeply of my essence. "I've never loved anyone this way before." Paul's kiss was deep and tender. I knew I had his heart, but it almost seemed too easy.

The evening moon had come up and the breeze off the lake sent us into the little cottage. We danced to a drowsy melody and something inside me lurched. I looked into his eyes to see if he had heard it. He smiled, oblivious to the murmur that was growing to a roar behind my eyes. I knew the evening would end, and we would have to say good-night. But I didn't want him to leave, not tonight. His hands reached out for me and a soft sound came out of my lips.

But then suddenly he reeled away from me.

*Why doesn't he want to touch me? Doesn't he find me desirable?* The roar inside my ears was deafening now. I looked in his eyes and dared him to love me, all of me. But while one woman raged in my soul, another one cried out.

Grabbing me by both arms, he stared at me, confused. His startled look did little to stop the roar and its command over me, but his honesty and compassion caught me off guard. For a moment the winds eased and I tried to come to grips with the question in my soul.

"I'm sorry, Paul ..." I tried to move away.

He held my hands firmly and did not let me shrink away. "Listen, Sarah Kay. I love you, but there is something here I have to reconcile with."

"What do you want?" I asked, my voice full of hurt and accusation.

"What do *you* want Sarah?" It wasn't his words but the look in his eyes that made me feel pitiful and used. I was a passionate person but that didn't make me defective. Mostly I've been persecuted as a prude. Except—but I was too young to know better ...

"Sarah, is there something you want to tell me?" His voice interrupted my thoughts.

As he prodded, the storm shrieked in my ears. *I am* not *damaged goods!* I curled defensively into a ball in front of him and rocked. I didn't hear what he said to me next, but I argued silently with him anyway: *I am still whole!* Doubt rose from the pit of my stomach. I could not escape him or his gaze. Yet what he was asking was humiliating. Confession was unthinkable. If I lied I would save him from ugly truth, and yet a piece of myself would be lost forever. But what if I told him? What was the truth? I'd been protecting myself for so long, I had never brought it before the Lord.

And then everything I had been holding in came tumbling out—every thought and word, every humiliating detail of my pubescent pain. The moments seemed to slow. I watched my words float out of my mouth, released like tangible figures. In the distance I could see the pained expression of his face, but I was transfixed. All I could focus on were the words as they flew out of my mouth. But the minute they crossed my lips it was as if the Lord himself had come in between us and caught every last one. The confession rose under God's forgiving gaze and disappeared into his wounded hands.

The storm stopped, a gentle peace was breathed into my soul, and somewhere deep inside a door opened. I heard a loving voice sigh and softly, gently thank me for finally letting go.

Another deeper, more haggard sigh broke my trance and I found my beloved boyfriend lying crumpled on the floor at my feet. "Paul!" He was lost somewhere between seething and sobbing. The minutes turned to hours, dotted with our heartbreaking conversation as we worked through the pain.

His grief was alarming. I'd never known someone who could care so deeply—but why? Was he hurting for me or for himself? "Were you ever planning to tell me?" he finally asked.

I couldn't understand. I was never abused or raped. I had just been too naïve as a teen, with slightly more "carnal knowledge" than I had wanted but nothing I had ever thought was serious. I was a virgin, a fact I was very proud of and had fought hard to protect.

As the self-pity crept into his voice, I couldn't stand it any longer. I had nothing left to say; this wasn't the man I knew. He had taken my vulnerability and swallowed it in his heart-wrenching sobs, but his sobs weren't for me. He seemed to be grieving his own loss. Too much had been said, and I rose to leave.

As I lay sleepless in my own bed, I fretted about what he said. Had he actually meant to propose this weekend? Was it over? He had taken every detail of my past and was suddenly holding it over my head. Could he do that? He seemed so wounded and yet he never reached out for *me*. His pain wasn't for my lost innocence, so what was it for? How could he judge me like that? I felt flush with emotion, but I couldn't cry, not tonight. Tonight I felt clean, new, and most of all, forgiven. That feeling outweighed them all.

Despite the difficulty of telling, something beautiful had come out of this emotional evening. I had spent so many years fighting for what innocence I still had, I had no idea that I held any pain for what I had lost. I had worked so hard to be pure, I was afraid to admit to any sin that had been ensnaring me. Things could have been different. But everything was forgiven, at least in my heart and with my Lord where it mattered most.

In the morning, Paul had risen early and sat by himself at the edge of the lake. The distance between us was evident. I was afraid for us, but somehow not for myself. I no longer felt I had anything to hide. I knew without a doubt that my ugly secrets didn't make God love me any less. What freedom! And no matter what, I had to be thankful that Paul's piety had brought me to my knees — the only place God could show me just how much he loved me.

When we finally did come face-to-face on the front porch of the cabin, Paul caught me off guard with the coldness in his eyes. Armed with all the doubts and differences, he began a long drawn out speech about forgiveness and virtue. I stood in front of him feeling like I was on trial all over again. It wasn't his words that spoke to me; it was his hurtful tone and angry eyes that told me where his heart was.

"Paul," I interrupted, "I'm sorry if you can't forgive me, but God has, and that's all that matters." I choked on my sudden tears and ran down the steps with the screen door slamming behind me, blindly running toward the lake. In a moment strong arms grabbed me and spun me around.

"Sarah, I'm so sorry, I'm so sorry." Paul sobbed but the softness in his eyes melted my heart instantly. "You were right. I hadn't forgiven you, not until you ran out that door and I realized how selfish I was being." Paul's words tumbled over each other, but I knew they were from the heart. Something new had been created in each of us and hope surged through me. We held each other as our tears mixed joyfully.

That wasn't our last battle. Both of us had different ideas about love, life, and service to God. But we knew that nothing could separate us.

≈ ≈

I have moments when tomorrow is on the tip of my tongue, and yesterday is still wrapped around my shoulders. Sometimes it comes in the shape of a season. And sometimes inspiration is veiled in another individual, someone who looks deep into your eyes and dares you to dream, to hope, to live. Paul was that person for me. I loved him for the healing and unsurpassing love he layered on my being.

Paul would be the first to tell you that I was that person for him too. He would smile and say that his life would have been so boring without me in the middle of it. I pushed him to try new things, discover new dreams, and live wildly outside the public eye. He would never have learned to dance, to cook, or to do countless other things that he did out of love for me.

Of course, there have been moments when I hated myself for being his muse. You see, I was the one who had been begging Paul to learn to ski. Without my encouragement, Paul wouldn't have considered skiing that fateful day. Some days I wish I could take a knife and remove the portions of my soul that love to fly and soar. If it weren't for the hand of God who brought us together so intimately and significantly, I think the guilt would have swallowed me whole. In my head I understand that an adventurous spirit isn't an imperfection, but in the face of Paul's pain it's only been the continuing whisper of God that has kept the demons at bay: "I didn't make a mistake when I created you."

One of my favorite stories about Jesus reminds me how much he loved broken people, especially those who questioned their worth or seemed to stand out in a crowd whether they wanted to or not.

*When one of the Pharisees invited Jesus to have dinner with him, he went to the Pharisee's house and reclined at the table. A woman in that town who lived a sinful life learned that Jesus was eating at the Pharisee's house, so she came there with an alabaster jar of perfume. As she stood behind him at his feet weeping, she began to wet his feet with her tears. Then she wiped them with her hair, kissed them and poured perfume on them.*

Luke 7:36–38

I love this story because of what isn't said, more than what is. As I imagine it, this is a Jewish woman who understood something of who God was, yet she had been forced into a gruesome and difficult life. Prostitution became her only option for survival. The things this woman had witnessed or been forced into make me want to weep for her and anyone in her position. I think of the leers, the horrible names, the way men had looked at her—like she was an animal without dignity or tenderness. My heart goes out to anyone treated this way.

She must have created such tall walls around her heart to protect her from the harsh realities of her life. She'd had no choice. If only someone had taken her in, been kind to her, protected her. Yet everywhere she turned, the world seemed cold and angry. It only wanted one thing from her. She was good only for prostituting her body, and because of that she was treated like dirt. This woman had been wronged by her society.

In Jesus' day, any pious Jew couldn't even touch this woman. She'd had intimate contact with the Romans and thus was considered "unclean." Yet on the day Jesus dined with the Pharisees, she boldly entered the house, braving ridicule, harassment, and possible stoning. Why did she come?

I believe it was Christ's eyes. It was the look in them that she had never seen before. In my short life I have had my fair share of lewd glances—the predatory look whose hunger and audacity seems to take away something pure. The woman at Christ's feet had witnessed so much worse than I could ever imagine, and yet there was something about this man—something so absolutely revolutionary that it would convince her she was special. She could approach this man and be forgiven. What a risk! How could she know? What if he turned her away? To risk any more heartbreak or judgment, she must have seen something so very different about Christ. Even though men had wronged her, used her, and abused her, this man was different.

I can't wait to meet this man, the one who could bring healing to such a broken heart. The gentle eyes of our Creator looking at his child, overwhelming her soul. Yes, she is a woman and she is beautiful to him in a pure, loving way. He knows her deeply, knows every detail of her soul, and he loves her. Christ not only accepts her form, her face, her soul, but he forgives her, releases her from her bondage of sin and suffering. If she could risk everything just to touch her Lord, believing that he would set her free, then what is holding me back?

When I think of what this woman says about Jesus, I want to fall on my knees and worship. I want to know this man myself. My foolish worries of life and womanhood all seem to fall away. Someday soon there will be healing at his feet, washing away the wounds of this world. All the pain and rejection will only be a faint memory. In this life I may experience the harsh end of reality, but someday soon I will be able to look into those eyes myself.

Chapter 7

# THE DAY *that* NEVER WAS

*Has this world been so kind to you that you should leave with regret?*
*There are better things ahead than any we leave behind.*
C. S. Lewis

"I think I can! I think I can! I think I can!" The words pound in my head as the rhythm of my feet pad along the pavement. "I think I can! I think I can!" I plod on, moving forward. The rhythm is natural now. Me, just me, without companion or roots, moving onward, trying to blend into my surroundings and yet always standing apart. My fifth city in a year and I am tired, so tired of moving. Once the mystery is gone and the newness has faded, it becomes just me, the consumer with a favorite shop or two. I love discovering a new place, learning its secrets, and becoming intimate with the local flavor. But money cannot buy roots. The world seems so much smaller. I may know the language, but no one knows my name. This time is no different. I am alone to wander. In my wanderings, I discover something. I am tired of wandering alone.

"Hello! Is anyone out there?" What is it about being with someone that makes the world so much more accessible, the faces friendlier, the images softer? With someone else, other people's laughter rolls past your ears; alone it accosts you. Alone, every detail is intense; existence is like living art. Laughter in the park, the couple holding hands, the reflection in the window—each image captures a masterpiece of normalcy. If you're quiet, you can hear the people growing older. Living, breathing, passing the time with no awareness of the preciousness of each moment.

My world is not romantic. When I moved alone to Chicago and tried to build a portion of the life that Paul and I had dreamed of, Paul was moved from a nursing home to his parent's house for round-the-clock care. Our lives were moving in opposite directions. I am trying to piece together a future without him. But every time I turn, something reminds me that this isn't the way it was supposed to be. It is only me to take out the trash, make coffee, change a lightbulb, and eat a meal.

I came across Paul's favorite sweater in my closet the other day. I took it out and slipped it over my frame. It was far too big, but a flood of memories came back as the smooth gray fibers brushed my skin: Paul's slightly stooped shoulders and long arms, his long lean form that looked sophisticated in the sleek masculine cut. I remember when we found it and how he fell in love with it instantly but didn't dare spend that much money on himself. I remember his face when he unwrapped it at Christmas.

I was hoping his sweater would bring me comfort, needing the feeling that I had made someone happy, that I had cared for someone and he was better because of me. The horrible thing about the accident is that Paul still needs the sweater to keep him warm, but he doesn't need me. Paul's sweet spirit will always remain, but little else is left.

The pounding of my feet on the sidewalk is the rhythm of life. I think I can! I think I can! I have escaped the four walls of my world, and the freedom has filled my head with thoughts of victory. I have done it! I have survived! I have outlived this monster named "Grief"! Today I know I have the strength to keep going. My feet keep moving and the world keeps turning.

Rounding the corner into my cozy courtyard, I smile at a lost-looking deliveryman. "Can I help you find something?" I ask. The fall air has filled me with exuberance.

"Ah, yes please," the man says taking a quick look at his clipboard.

"I'm looking for 27, Apartment 4a."

"That's my apartment," I say in surprise.

"Are you Sarah Kay?" he asks.

I nod dumbly.

"Then these are for you." He proudly hands me a huge bouquet of the most beautiful flowers I have seen in a long time—along with a pen with which to accept delivery.

"Oh my gosh. Thank you," I stammer, unable to think who would send me such amazing flowers.

"Strange day to send flowers. Is it your birthday?" he asks as I fumble with the pen.

"No, it's not my birthday. Why do you call it a strange day?" I ask curiously.

The unnamed man looks at me like I've lost my mind and then rolls his eyes before walking away. "Um, it's September eleventh?" he calls out over his shoulder, leaving me standing in my doorway speechless.

Suddenly I understand the look on the man's face. How could I not realize that today is the anniversary of a national tragedy? Little does he know that today is also the anniversary of a lesser-known tragedy. Entering my apartment I find a place for the glorious bouquet and search the foliage for a card, wondering who would think to send me flowers on this date.

You don't know me, but I knew Paul. He became so special to me over the years that he came to my shop. In fact, he and I created the bouquet he gave you the day he proposed. You have been in my prayers ever since I heard about the accident. I know how much Paul loved you, and I couldn't let today pass without sending you some of my love and his.

I sink into a nearby chair as it all comes flooding back. "Happy Today!" Paul would proclaim as he proudly held out a colorful bouquet of whatever flowers had caught his eye that day. But today isn't just any other day. It is special.

Two years ago today, I awoke with a smile. It was *my* day. Full of hope and possibility. Paul had been working weekends and nights at the store, but today we had the rare chance to spend the day together. I ran down the stairs of the cozy little Cape Cod that I shared with six of my dearest friends, all of us seniors. Each of my roommates kissed me on the cheek as she left, sharing in my joy. Paul and I had a wonderful breakfast together, reveling in the unique quiet.

We switched on the radio as he took me to class, and we heard a nervous newscaster claim that an airliner had crashed into one of the Twin Towers of the World Trade Center.

"Is this someone's idea of a sick joke?" Paul asked in disbelief.

He dropped me off at my class, and I moved in slow motion. Classes had been canceled and students were pouring out of the chapel where they had gathered for prayer. It was almost noon as I stumbled from a TV screen in the college commons looking for a familiar face. When Elisa saw me, I threw myself into her arms, sobbing.

We held on to each other in a daze. We both felt shock and sorrow. It was unbelievable to think of so much death on our own soil. As we walked the few blocks home, neighbors were standing on their front lawns talking with each other. It was odd to walk through the quiet neighborhoods and see businessmen returning from the city early. Most of the taller office buildings had been evacuated, and Paul was scrambling since he had planned to propose at the John Hancock Center on the shores of Lake Michigan that very evening.

After the shock had worn off and we had taken time to pray for our nation and the thousands of people affected by this evil, I selfishly felt the sting of tragedy simply because of what the day was supposed to be for Paul and me. My mind kept going back to the date I'd inscribed on the gift I was planning to give Paul that evening. "Why now? Why today?" I wondered miserably.

It was the one-year anniversary of the infamous jazz concert that had started it all. So much had happened in those twelve months. Walking through Wheaton I had noticed a gift in the window of a downtown shop that I thought would be perfect for Paul. It was a money clip with a clock on it. I knew it would be a perfect anniversary present, so I had meaningful words engraved on it:

> "I thank my God at every remembrance of thee."
> I love you, Paul.
> September 11th 2001

Paul was taking me out to dinner, but I had asked him not to get me anything else. I knew his budget was tight. Still, I wanted to do something for him to honor this day. Little did I know that Paul had been planning for months to ask me to marry him on September eleventh. He had honored my request for us to experience four seasons side-by-side, but he couldn't wait a minute longer to ask me to be his bride. Paul had called my parents the night before and asked them for their blessing. They were thrilled at the thought of having Paul in our family and had wholeheartedly consented.

Now stunned and confused by the national disaster, he had returned home to consult his roommate and to make several calls to our families, looking for guidance but also wanting to hear their voices in the midst of such an awful tragedy.

They urged him to continue with his plan, but it was George W. himself who helped Paul make the final decision. The president, in a passionate speech that afternoon, urged the country not to let the terrorists win by drawing back in fear. Paul hoped to make something beautiful out of this tragic day and decided to go forth with his original plan.

Instead of heading into the city, Paul and I found a cozy Italian restaurant in Geneva, Illinois, where Paul ran a growing business. A small crowd had braved the night, and we listened to beautiful jazz music and glided across the dance floor of the restaurant's classy little club. It was a magical night full of romance, and the day's horrors seemed so far away.

We wandered out into the summer air, flush with love, and found ourselves in an adorable lit courtyard that looked like it belonged in an Italian villa. As beautiful music wrapped around us, I stopped and closed my eyes. I wanted to capture this feeling.

"Sarah Kay," Paul's voice lilted into my reverie. "You know how much I love you and what an amazing woman I think you are. And I'm not the only one who thinks so. My parents have been praying for the woman that I was going to marry for years." As the words sank in, I opened my eyes to see Paul kneeling before me holding a little box.

"Sarah Kay, I want to spend the rest of my life with you. Would you marry me?"

I felt my heart rise to my throat and my knees felt weak. There weren't words to express what I was feeling in that moment, so I nodded my head as a huge smile broke across my face. Paul slipped the beautiful bauble onto my finger, stood, and drew me into a passionate embrace. As we parted, I tried to breathe. I didn't want my first words to my new fiancé to be, "I want to sit down," so I breathlessly whispered, "I love you. I have to sit down."

We sat and prayed a brief thank you to God for bringing us together, and then I called my parents to share our good news. It was beautiful to have something to celebrate, even on September 11, 2001.

≈ ≈

Today I stare at the flowers I've just received and wonder again what to do with anniversaries—not just with the remembrances of special days, but of the event that never happened. June 29, 2002 was supposed to be my wedding day, the day I was to marry Paul Olson in my home church in front of two hundred of our closest friends.

Some days I don't know if I am living in the present or the past. So many sights and sounds that come back—like specters, they creep and I am at their mercy. To dwell in the past, to remain true to the memories, is that commendable? Or should I move forward, gradually building my life anew without pieces of yesterday? But how can I be so heartless?

Time marches on whether I like it or not. If I had my way, September 11 and June 29 would have been permanently erased from the calendars; we would skip from Wednesday to Friday, and out of respect, no one would say a word. Maybe it could be a bank holiday, retire the number somehow.

Selfishness consumes me, selfishness and shame. I made us wait until June to marry (Paul had wanted to get married in February but I resisted). I am the one who kept the sweater for myself while he's the one who should have it. I am the one who moved away from him. I am the one who has gone on with my life. The broken and marred form in Paul's place causes such broad emotions in me that I've stayed away from him, afraid of myself. Afraid that it was ugly to withhold my love. Can love die when our bodies stay alive? How can I ever hope to forgive myself for leaving him when he was so broken?

If I ever marry again, I tell myself, everything will be done differently than what Paul and I intended for our wedding. The events we had planned for June twenty-ninth will stay locked away in my heart. It's not much of a promise, nothing noble, but I will be adamant. Nothing can ever replace the day that should have been or the man who was just getting started.

My running clothes are starting to stick to me, and I step away from the flowers and move toward the shower. But guilt doesn't wash off as easily as sweat. I need more than water.

I slip into comfortable sweats and cradle a steaming coffee cup in my hand. In the stillness of my urban apartment, I stare at the unopened Bible resting on my lap. I guess my unwillingness to open my Bible is a sign of how I feel God slipping further and further away from me. A rift grows between God and me, and I don't know how to bridge it. I look at the flowers, knowing that I forgot what today was, and I wonder wistfully if I really deserve God's grace.

In my new quiet existence I have been trying to rebuild some semblance of life in the aftermath of loss. I have struggled to find perspective and hope in the ashes of what could have been. I have learned firsthand that tragedy and joy coexist alongside a loving

Lord who never forsakes his people, even when he allows suffering. But at this point, it is something I need to *feel*, not just understand.

In the midst of my quiet desperation, I plead with God for some type of reassurance that he hasn't forgotten me. Paul had been an aspiring pastor, and together we had committed our lives in service to God. No matter how strong my faith, I admit I am mystified that the Lord chose to take him from me only four months before our wedding and leave him in that semi-comatose state. Today, Paul is silent to the world and our future lies shattered in a thousand pieces. Questions plague me. How could something so beautiful become so tragic? Have I misread the Lord's will? Is this some colossal mistake?

These thoughts hadn't tormented me in the past two years, and I'm surprised that a voice from the past could trigger so much doubt.

I place the flowers beside my computer and sit down to write. I write to my unseen audience of hope and despair. Clarity and redemption come on the pages that grow under my fingers. I rarely understand the steps I have made or why I have to plod forward, and yet on the pages I pour out my torment, hoping that the paper will record my pain and thus forgive me my selfishness.

I live while he is silent. I laugh while he is broken. How can one ever explain or understand the injustice of life? Who among us has a right to cast the first stone? Certainly not me. Survival has a price and I would gladly give my pound of flesh to have the debt removed. Who am I to ever smile again?

June twenty-ninth will always be a day of remembrance, my day of mourning and joy. Instead of remembering the accident, I will remember the life, even if I hold to memories of what should have happened instead of what did. On this day, all my ambitions and hopes will be gone. The specters of the past will win and I will concede to them this day. It'll be like a game of chess—I will make a move for a wholesome, productive day; some days I will win, some days I will lose.

➶ ➷

It was less than two years ago that I honored Paul and publicly declared my love for him. On the day we were to be married, instead of fading from his life, I committed my life to him. Instead of two hundred of our friends and family gathering in a festively decorated church, two dozen brave and gentle souls gathered in an open room of the County Hospital. Unable to let the day go by silently, I hoped to touch some of the joy that Paul and I had shared and to warm myself with its memory.

Unavoidable sadness was in the air as I slipped my engagement ring from my finger and replaced it with a solid silver band bearing the Hebrew characters that pledged, "I am my beloved's and he is mine." I had not known a better time to remove my engagement ring with any less honor and dignity than it deserved. I placed it in its original box and set it aside, not knowing when I would have the heart to look at it again.

My ring, like our relationship, was unique, beautiful, and given to us by the Lord. Paul, being an intense romantic and old-fashioned in his beliefs, had declared his intentions to me on our first "official" date. Being a year younger than my handsome Paul, I was slightly more hesitant of talking about marriage and asked that we walk through four seasons together. As time went on, Paul and I grew closer and deeper in our faith and commitment to each other. Paul was incredibly passionate, devoted, and creative, and each season was filled with prayer and blissful romance.

In the spring of 2001, as Paul was preparing to graduate from Wheaton College, I had found myself with one of my best friends, Elisa, at a jewelry store, feasting my eyes on the sparkly solitaires that winked at me from their cases. Even in the excitement, all the traditional settings seemed to look alike and indistinctive to my idealistic eye — until I stumbled onto a ring I couldn't take my eyes off of. It had a gold band with a solitary diamond, and yet it was so unusual, it wasn't even in the wedding section of the store. I was hooked. It looked amazing on my finger and made me feel giddy. But falling in love with this unique bauble presented a problem. How could I admit to my romantic Paul that I had simply stumbled upon my engagement ring without him? I had such peace about this distinct ring and yet, with determination, I walked out of the store and put it out of my head.

≈ ≈

Paul knew I loved surprises, so he always kept any talk of his romantic plans far from my ears. You can imagine my surprise then when he invited me to go engagement ring shopping. Since it was only eight months into our courtship, I wanted to be sure this was the appropriate step for us, so I prayed for a sign. The Lord had been so tender and direct in our relationship, and I prayed our actions would honor him. A sign would be confirmation and would allow me assurance that we were still being true to him and not being hasty.

With joy and nervousness, we began the day with a picnic and prayer. Always the romantic, Paul had a huge bouquet of flowers for me "just because." I had incredible peace in my spirit as we made our first stop. As we browsed, both of us seemed mildly impressed by the vast selection of stones and bands that all seemed to resemble each other — until we came to a ring that had certain unique features that caught both our eyes. Paul studied the ring and began a discussion with the jeweler about custom making something with slight differences. As he talked and eventually sketched his idea on the back of a handy business card, I watched and felt a chill run down my spine. The ring he was describing was an exact replica of the ring I had fallen in love with months before.

"Which one of my friends have you been talking to?" I inquired incredulously. Tingling with excitement, we moved on to another shop. As we entered, I realized that it was the same place I had been so enthusiastically play-shopping months before. I confessed sheepishly that I had been in there earlier, mere seconds before the store clerk blurted out that she remembered me! I checked my embarrassment and scolded myself for my girlish behavior as I inched in the direction of the engagement rings. That ring wouldn't be here, I thought to myself. It was months ago.

At that same exact moment, Paul stopped and pointed to a glinting shape in the case below him, remarking, "That's the ring I've been picturing in my head."

Stifling a gasp, I realized what he was pointing to. Without hesitation, and out of the hundreds of gems surrounding us, Paul had been drawn to the exact ring I had found months before! *Okay, Lord*, I thought. *You've made your point perfectly clear. If that's not a sign, I don't know what is.*

≈ ≈

I get up from the computer and dig up the familiar box. A little afraid, I crack it open and look at my beautiful ring. Our love story, the story of how this ring came into my possession, seems to mock my insecurities about God, love, and life. How could I have been given this ring that was so clearly not going to be a symbol of our lifelong devotion?

As I study every unique feature that had drawn me to it a lifetime ago, I muse about the symbolism of the wedding ring as the unending bond of love between a man and a woman. Suddenly, like a gust of wind, the Holy Spirit seems to run his gentle fingers across my gaze. As if seeing my engagement ring with new eyes, I notice something I hadn't seen before. With most wedding rings, it's their perfect shape that signifies the bond of commitment. With no end and no beginning, the roundness is a symbol of purity and faithfulness. But my ring isn't a perfect circle. My ring is a single strip of gold, wrapping around my finger and coming to two distinct parallel points, only to be joined by a single pure diamond.

A slow smile creeps over my face. God loves me so much, he even planned the perfect ring to celebrate Paul's and my unique, unconsummated love. This band of gold has a distinct beginning and end, as well as a perfectly clear glint of the diamond holding the two pieces together. Where before I had seen broken promises and shattered dreams, now I see a faithful God who tenderly makes sure he never misleads me. By choosing a unique symbol for our unique situation, he was even making sure that my token of love was perfect, in keeping with his perfect, if not incomprehensible, plan.

This lesson from an intimately personal God is a stunning reminder that, in the Lord's delicate and loving way, he gave Paul and me a special and needed token for our distinctive relationship. I place the ring on my right hand to serve as a constant reminder of his intimate commitment to the details of my life and heart.

The body can naturally grieve for only so long. Smiles must return, even through tears. It is the natural purging of pain. To laugh is to live, but laughter is formed in pain. Laughter is the natural complement to pain. It's the consolation prize and a rite of passage, and I know that someday I will see Paul laughing.

Chapter 8

# COMING HOME

*Memory is a way of holding on to the things you love,*
*the things you are, the things you never want to lose.*
*The Wonder Years*

*I*t's early Saturday morning. An eerie fog, unusual for this time of year, blankets the sleeping city. I have nowhere to go, but I climb into my sporty white Solara anyway. I just can't bear to be in my empty apartment a moment longer. I have no destination, so I meander through the empty town, past cemeteries and civic centers, past grocery stores and movie theaters. The sun is breaking and trying to melt the mist. I can't see far ahead, but at least now I can drive between the lines. Perhaps listening to classical music in the eerie dawn provokes me to construct thoughtful analogies because I'm comparing the last few years of my life to this little road trip. It's been such a clumsy road, long and winding. The fog is still lifting. I've never had a clear view at any point.

Even now, I'm not sure what to do. Two and a half years after the accident, God again has me on my face before him, pleading for my life, for wholeness, for direction. Paul has started to respond slightly through simple hand gestures. After two years of silence, it is incredible to watch. The doctors in their wisdom had told us that two years would mark the end of any improvements that Paul

131

would be capable of, but God in his infinite wisdom will not be confined to man's timeline. It is amazing to see Paul's vacant looking form start to respond to commands and to see small bits of old movements that were so true to his personality. I wish I could say I rejoice completely in these moments, but seeing those little bits of Paul without truly communicating rips me in two with anguish.

No matter how thankful I am to see any sign of life in Paul, his progress unleashes a torrent of tears even when I don't think I can cry anymore. Lord, how do I love this man? I have failed Paul in so many ways, and yet still I can't touch him and truly cross the divide that separates us. Paul's injury has robbed me of my love and robbed me of my choice. If standing beside Paul is simply a matter of choice, you must believe it would be mine. But choice has little to do with our future, no matter how much I fight or how much he loved. The silence of brokenness has smothered our choices. Reality was not kind to us. It wasn't gentle — it was messy and frightening.

I have moved away from him not out of choice but simply out of survival. Yet now everything has been ripped open again. Was I wrong? Have I made a mistake? I rush to Paul's side, hopeful but terrified.

God what do you want from me?

Although Paul isn't silently sleeping, peacefully communing with the Lord, he's also not restored by any stretch of the imagination. Instead his body continues to groan and grapple with its severe impairments; it is difficult to measure how much he comprehends and how much he simply performs. Paul's progress is sweet, but not complete. Again I bow to medical jargon; again I release my hope for companionship. I am simply glad that his humanity and his dignity are now evident. Paul is progressing, but it isn't for me. No matter what I hope for, Paul is God's. Paul's family continues to surround him, and little Piper now gleefully crawls into her brother's lap and moves his hands so he can play with whatever toy she's playing with.

Some days I wish someone had given me a manual of directions. When do you say good-bye? How do you love anything or anybody when you're positive your heart has shrunk and shriveled up into nothingness?

During my deepest heartache I just wanted someone to tell me what to do, to map out the right and wrong from the gray haze that was my world. But no one could. I was a fledgling grown-up —young enough to be confused but old enough to take care of myself. Sorrow and grief are like a maze, every turn and corner seems to lead you nowhere, and your sense of direction has been scrambled with the rest of your insides. But it's your maze, your life; no one else can move forward but you, no matter how terrible it seems. I think recovery from tragedy is called survival because that's all that is expected—to make it through alive. That's all I did for a while.

⁓ ⁓

Looking back, I wish I would have done so many things differently. The stronger me would have called more, written more, visited more to anyone and everyone. I would have had more patience and forgiveness. In the middle of my maze I felt cut off from everyone in my past and my present. I would let the answering machine do my talking for days on end. I would walk down the corner for pizza only when I was so hungry I shook.

Friendships are like plants; they need to be watered and fed regularly. A plant never gets mad at you for neglect but eventually it begins to show wear. Oh, how I wish I had all my friends with me nearby, or something that would have made it easier for me to give them the love they deserved. Now as life begins to right itself, it's the secondary wounds that I notice, the aftereffects of the accident.

Tired and alone, I call home. I know my mom will be there. Like always. The hardiest plant of them all.

"Something's wrong, Sarah Kay," she tells me after I greet her wearily.

I can't keep my heartache from my mother. I don't even try this morning. I tell her my silly analogy and share with her my feelings of loneliness.

"Come home, honey," she says. "Right now. Just turn your car in my direction, and come straight here. I have an idea." One thing I can always say for my mother is that she never waits for a problem to fix itself. No matter how bold or impossible, she'll find a way to solve it.

Thankful for a place to go, I turn my car around and head my gypsy self home. It isn't the first time I've made an impetuous road trip, heading west. As white lines tick off the miles underneath me, my mind slips into a memory.

☙ ❧

"It won't start?" I asked incredulously. The voice on the other end of the phone belonged to my childhood friend Renee. Together we had backpacked Siberia and Arkansas before we graduated from high school. Now our adventurous plans for a long weekend in Chicago had gone up in smoke along with Renee's alternator. I couldn't help but feel sorry for myself. A senior in college with an impending four-day break, I had been looking forward to one more crazy story to add to my montage of college memories.

"Now I'm going to be so bored," I pouted to Paul. "And you'll be working most of the weekend!" The frame shop he managed was his pride and joy, but the start-up store demanded all his attention and most of his free time.

"You'll be fine," he assured me. "You've been complaining about all the millions of things you never get around to. Well, here's your chance."

I accepted this rationale and kissed him good-bye. "See you in a few days, Paul."

After Paul left I wandered into the kitchen to find Elisa saying good-bye to her boyfriend over the phone. High school sweethearts, the couple had reunited late in our college career even though they were several states apart.

"You know what's worse than a long-distance relationship?" she asked frustrated.

"Having six girls in a house and only one phone?" I ventured, trying to cheer her up. She wasn't the only girl in our picturesque Cape Cod who had a boyfriend on the other side of the country, and phone time had become a common complaint.

"Close," she replied cracking a smile. "But even worse is having a long-distance boyfriend and a long weekend with no possibility of seeing each other."

"I thought you were going to go see him," I commiserated, secretly glad that someone else would be left in the house this weekend.

"I tried, but I couldn't get a good price on a flight, and he's leading worship on Sunday so he can't get away either." It was obvious from the romantic packages that had been arriving on our doorstep ever since these two had become an item again that feelings between them ran deep. But Elisa was levelheaded and Erik was laid-back, and strong emotion was rarely shared openly, so the disappointment in her eyes caught me off guard.

I felt guilty for my moment of selfishness and knew just how to make it up to her. "You know what would make you feel better?" I offered. "Let's get dressed up and go out."

"What'll we do?"

"I don't care if all we do is go to the mall," I told her. "But we're going to get gorgeous! The better you look, the better you'll feel. Am I right?"

Laughing, Elisa agreed. We were still little girls at heart, and after an hour of messing around in each other's closets, we were ready to take on the town. The mood had already lifted considerably. Once on the highway I began to lament to her about my weekend plans and how I had been looking forward to having some fun.

"You know," mused my calm, calculating friend, "if we left right now we could be in Virginia in time for church."

I just stared at her. Elisa and I had road-tripped across America before, but not without careful planning.

"Don't tell me you're not up for a spontaneous idea," she said, laughing.

She was serious. I guess anything is possible when properly motivated. I hesitated for a moment, going over the practical rationale I had drafted earlier in the evening, but she blew away all my reservations with her next sentence.

"I can pay for gas. I'm just glad to have someone keep me company. And once we get to Virginia, Erik's mother will take care of everything else. She's hilarious and an incredible hostess."

She knew she had me in the bag. How could I refuse a free cross-country road trip? I didn't have to be back in class till Wednesday. Besides, I couldn't let Elisa show me up when it came to spontaneity. "I'm in! Let's just run back and grab a couple of things and we're gone!" I said feeling the elation that comes with possibility.

"Oh, no. If we do that we'll lose an hour and it will take us twelve just to get there. There's no time to go back."

Stunned at her heroic attitude and not being one to complain, I jumped on board. "Okay, but we need to at least stop and get a map and a camera."

"Why a camera?" she asked, switching lanes toward the off-ramp.

"Oh, honey, a trip like this must be documented," I replied like the old pro that I was. Fifteen minutes later we had a route mapped out and Abdul, the cashier at the gas station, had snapped the first picture of our long, long night.

Somewhere between twelve thirty and Ohio, Paul's roommate, Annika's fiancé, Eric, spilled the beans of my antics, and when Paul called Elisa's cell phone, it sounded more like a prison break than college camaraderie.

"Hi Paul! Guess what?" I squeaked with a nervous giggle.

"Sarah, where are you?" Paul demanded with aggravation in his voice.

"Well, I was going to make you guess, but at the moment I'm not sure where we are. Where are we?" I whispered holding the phone to my chest.

"Toledo," Elisa whispered back.

"We're in Toledo. I mean, we're passing Toledo. We're not staying here, we're just driving through," I stammered.

"Elisa invited me to her boyfriend's house for the weekend. I know it's a little spur-of-the-moment, but she needed someone to keep her awake and I didn't have anything else to do."

"You didn't have anything else to do?" Paul sounded hurt and annoyed. "I thought you and I were going to church together tomorrow? When were you going to tell me?"

"Okay, poor choice of words; I didn't mean I had nothing to do, and I was going to call you first thing in the morning. I thought it would be funnier that way."

"I don't think it's funny that I had to find out from Eric, who heard it from Annika, like you were running away. SK, we talked about this and decided that you were going to stay home this weekend."

"Okay, I'm sorry, that does seem childish. We're just having fun, Paul. It just feels really good to get away, a change of scenery, you know."

"No, I don't know, Sarah. What did you need to get away from? Me?"

"Of course not, Paul. Sometimes I just get stir-crazy. You know this about me."

"Yeah, we've talked about it, but are you going to do this when we're married with kids at home, just run away when you feel 'stir-crazy'?"

"Paul, that's not fair. I'm in college and I'm just having some fun."

"Oh, and being with me isn't fun? I don't know, Sarah. I'm very disappointed. I can't talk about this anymore tonight. I'll call you tomorrow."

"Paul, wait. Hello ... Paul? I can't believe it! He hung up on me," I stared at the phone in my hand.

"I'm sorry, SK. I didn't mean to cause you any trouble," Elisa looked at me sympathetically.

"Oh Elisa, it's not your fault. I just feel like I'm in the sixth grade or something. I suppose I would have been ticked if I'd heard from one of you that my fiancé had taken off."

I was confused and frustrated at my own behavior. I guess deep down, part of me was fearful that if I had called him when

I was still on the move, I might have been talked into turning around. Paul had a way of "out-spiritualizing" me. His reasoning was sound and his motives pure, but his childhood hadn't included anything this rash. In a moment when I had been incredibly true to myself—impetuosity and all—I had caused a huge rift in our relationship.

I wasn't used to this type of reaction and had little understanding of what I had done wrong. My reaction from home was completely opposite. Announcing my destination to my mother, she'd laughed in delight. I had been a life-loving, headstrong thrill-seeker since before I could drive, and all these attributes had allowed me to do amazing things for God all over the world.

Arriving in Virginia just in time for breakfast, the Palmer family laughed in surprise but happily took us in. And Erik, of course, was thrilled. Later that year he admitted that the very weekend we showed up on his doorstep unannounced, he'd been praying for a sign confirming that the time was right for him and Elisa to get married.

But by the time we returned home, Paul and I had had many tearful conversations, and I had never felt more wronged. I knew he was hurt because I'd taken off without him, but his anger also revealed a huge gap between our worlds. Paul loved me and sometimes knew me better than I knew myself, but sometimes it felt like there just wasn't much room in his reality for the woman he loved. Sometimes, the extra pieces of myself seemed to stick out of the mold of "Christian woman" and neither of us knew what to do with them.

🦅 🦅

I notice that the fog is completely gone and I'm halfway home. I feel bad for spending time in the memory I've just conjured. Perhaps

I should remember Paul like a storybook character, perfect in every way. But Paul wasn't perfect. He was human. Besides, as they say, a person's greatest weakness is also his greatest strength. Still, being honest about the mistakes of our past makes it harder and harder for me to believe in our future. Now that so much time has passed, I wonder if the woman I am now would fall for Paul. I wonder if Paul would have been better off without falling for me. Shaking my head to clear my thoughts, I decide that I don't need to revise history. The fact is, we will never have the chance to live out our days together, but nothing can take away those days we did have. I will remember him honestly. I'm thankful for every bit of life I had with the sweet boy-turned-man. I loved Paul, flaws and all, just as he loved me. Our mistakes as much as our successes made us lovable. Without our blemishes we could never understand how it feels to be loved unconditionally.

I will remember him, but whenever the fog closes in and my memories get muddled, I will return to the colorful cigar box where I've stashed pieces of my life with Paul: bits of his writings to me, a ticket stub to a jazz concert, a card, a poem, and some dried blue rose petals.

꧁ ꧂

I dreamt wildly and prayed even more passionately and the Lord brought me a man who loves to hear me laugh, loves to carry me over snowbanks, and hates to miss church (it was almost like our date). He gave me a man whose heart beats after him, a man who needs me to coax him, remind him, introduce him to others who will invite him to preach. A man who brings out the little girl in me, who lets me laugh at myself and still thinks I'm amazing. Who brings me flowers for no reason and loves to read to me. A man who is an intensely hard worker and plays just as passionately.

Who gets frustrated when women want to wear the pants in the relationship but loves my feisty strong side. Who loves to see me make a mess when I cook but would live on grilled cheese for the rest of his life if he had to cook. Paul loves my friends so much that he would spend an entire two weeks with their boyfriends, fiancés, and husbands, dreaming up an early Valentine's show and formal event for us.

≈ ≈

After one of Paul's beautiful spectacles of devotion, I wondered what he wanted to do for the actual Valentine's Day. He was wonderful about surprising me with flowers, just because. "Happy Today," he called these spontaneous holidays, borrowing the term from his toddler sister. But I knew that Valentine's Day scared Paul to death. He claimed his father had never been a good gift giver and was intimidated by the commercialization of the holiday. I, on the other hand, had spent several Valentine's Days shopping for one beau or another and wanted to show Paul that I cared in a heartfelt manner. As a missionary child in Africa, I had learned to knit as a requirement of my international education. Now years later, I had picked it up again with my roommate, and we were clumsily turning out scarves and hats in a variety of colors as fast as our untrained fingers would go.

I was attempting to finish a pale blue scarf for Paul, made of the softest yarn I could find, knowing that it would go so well with his brown leather jacket. But finding the time to knit when he wasn't around had been the difficult part. Paul seemed constantly on my case about how hard I was working and how wound up I was getting.

"Just take five minutes for yourself to relax," he would encourage, but I was beyond stressed. My class load had intensified, and between student government and a part-time job, having a boy-friend was the last thing I'd planned on. And yet over the past few months, Paul and I had become inseparable. Partly out of necessity, we had taken some of the same classes and were studying together, something that played a bit negatively on my sense of independence, but he was smart and very helpful. He would meet me before class, brief me on the reading I hadn't had time to prepare, and I would discuss it knowledgably during class as if I was a politician briefed on the talking points of the day. It was often our own bit of humor, but there were days I didn't know how to build the appropriate boundaries. It didn't hurt that we adored each other, but it didn't help that I never seemed to have enough time to study.

As Valentine's night rolled around, I was up in my tower inside the brick walls of Williston, frantically trying to knit and read the next day's assignment, when the phone rang.

It was Paul. He had given me most of the afternoon but now wanted me to join him for the evening. I made up an excuse or two. Always a passionate soul but rarely one to lose his temper, Paul's voice rose a notch or two.

"Well, excuse me for wanting to see my girlfriend on Valentine's Day!" he hissed.

"Oh really," I answered haughtily, frustrated and at the end of my rope. "Well, if you must know what I'm doing," I hissed back, "I'm trying to finish your present! But since you never leave me alone, I haven't had a chance!"

I assumed by the silence on the other end that my words had hit home. The minute I said it, I knew that my frustration had merely boiled over, but this was not how I wanted to spend my Valentine's Day. "I'll be right down, Paul," I sighed. "Give me a minute." Without ceremony, I placed half of the scarf into a gift bag with the needles still attached and headed downstairs. The scarf didn't have to be perfect and neither did Valentine's Day.

But I wish I could say that either of us had learned our lesson. Later that same spring, I received a similar frustrated phone call from a very put-out Paul. "I've been trying my best to make time for you this last week and all you do is put me off. What's going on, SK?" he grumbled.

Here we were again. I was trying to get work done, trying to balance life and love without much luck. But this time I had had enough. "Paul, I don't think you're hearing me! I need time to get things done. I also need time to myself—time to breathe!"

"That's really not what I wanted to hear, Sarah. I was hoping that by now you'd know how to make us a priority."

"Well, look who knows so much!" I grumbled. "If you're so enlightened, you would know that I hadn't forgotten you. In fact, I was planning on making it up to you this weekend. I've been planning a surprise picnic for us all week. I've been looking forward to spending that time with you and trying to get done with other stuff so I could focus on you! But you just can't wait, can you? Did you really think I was so heartless?"

Now anyone who knows me well knows that I have a tendency to avoid conflict until I snap and it all bubbles to the surface. That night it came out like a gusher. Feeling vindicated by the fact that I was trying to plan something nice for Paul, a torrent of resentment went over the phone lines to my stunned boyfriend.

Mortified, Paul tried to apologize, but something in me had been waiting for a moment like this and I railed. I felt like he hadn't been respectful of me or my other relationships, even though I had asked him several times. We went back and forth, but I was forti-fied by my anger and ended the call definitively by saying, "I need my space to think about this. Hmmph! I don't know if we're sup-posed to be together if you can't learn to respect me, Paul."

Neither of us slept well that night, and in the morning my anger turned to dread. What had I done? Did I make a mistake? Surely

Paul would find me today and apologize. When I saw him, I'd know better what I was feeling. But I didn't see him, not that morning or even that evening. This man who had been a permanent fixture in my dorm had suddenly vanished. Now this was something I hadn't expected, and as I returned to my dorm I did the only thing a girl could do at a moment like that. I called my mom.

As fate would have it, Paul and I weren't the only ones at odds that night. I could hear frustration in my mother's voice when I explained my dilemma.

"Honey," she said, "I'm in the doghouse with your father right now and it's not fun. You and your dad are so similar. You hold things in so much that the rest of us are forced to live on pins and needles while you get it out of your system. Sarah, don't throw all this away over something so foolish. Call your boyfriend!"

Within minutes, my trembling hands had dialed Paul's number. I had always been a stubborn soul, so this alone was a humbling move. Paul was very surprised to hear my voice on the line but relief crept over both of us. It turns out, in a fit of remorse, Paul had left school to go to a Bible conference in Chicago that day and had just returned home. "I missed you today," I confessed.

"That's so good to hear, SK. I admit I thought this was it for us. I wasn't sure I would ever hear from you." Obviously my stubborn streak was common knowledge and I blushed sheepishly. "Well, I got some good advice," I mumbled.

That Saturday morning as Paul walked into my dorm with a fistful of blue roses, he was greeted with a smile from another young man familiar to the place. "Ah ... 'I'm sorry' flowers?" he smiled knowingly.

Paul always knew how to find just the right flower for the occasion and we laughed as I got a blue petal stuck to the bottom of my shoe. "It looks like I stepped on a smurf!" I exclaimed. Watching him laugh was one of the sweetest sights I could imagine. As we sat on a blanket in the park, Paul looked at me thoughtfully.

"You know that I'm so sorry for how I've smothered you recently, but babe, there's something I have to ask you." I looked up from my muffin in surprise and concern. "Well, hon, you know I'm gonna mess up again, no matter how much I care for you, but I have to know that it's not going to be like this every time."

"What do you mean?" I asked, puzzled.

"You know that I'm serious about us, and that I want us to grow together, and so I'm thinking about our future when I say that I worry that, well, that every time we get into an argument, you'll threaten to break up with me."

Bang! His question went straight to my heart. I had never had someone understand my behavior before or call me on it like this. Just as quickly, I also realized that I had indeed gotten into the bad habit of cutting my dates off at the knees when they stepped on my toes or disrespected me in any way. But in the past it had been a healthy defense mechanism. After all, it had kept the riffraff away. And yet it was possible that the time for such violent reactions had come to an end. Paul and I were going to have to work for our relationship, not against it, right? Wow, did he have me figured out. And yet without malice or judgment, he'd tenderly reached out to me in spite of myself. Only a few days after I was questioning our future, I was suddenly realizing how strong our present had become. In his honest question was a man who wanted to build something with me that would last. I must have been incredibly stunned by this new line of thought because after we returned to the van, I managed to smack my head against the steel frame with a vengeance. My lumpy bruise was a reminder of my out-of-place hardheadedness. But hey, it got me out of doing the dishes that day.

〜 〜

Memorabilia has powerful effects. For Paul, his strong desire to be my prince was portrayed in a gift from his mother—a glass cup displaying a cartoon of a boy holding a flower; the caption read, "Waiting for my princess." As a symbol of his mother's love for me and to welcome me into the family, Paul's mother had given me a little toy statue, a white knight in full regalia. On his shield, cloak, and flag was the image of a swan.

And Paul met those expectations. He had been my gregarious knight who would slay dragons and leap to my rescue. He lived out his favorite song, "Hero," by Enrique Iglesias by lavishing me with his protective love. He was the handsome prince who swept me off my feet—though one blustery night, my friends might have said he was the dragon who stole me away.

〜 〜

The snow crunched beneath my feet as I ran through the biting wind toward my dorm. I was so very late. I'd planned to watch a movie with the girls and was, in their minds, committing the worst sin: ditching out to be with a boy. But Paul had surprised me with something beautiful that night, and I clamored down the stairs toward my expectant friends, hoping I could express what had just happened. I was breathless with the cold and overflowing emotion as I peeked into the cozy sitting room where my best friends were curled up watching a movie.

I knew they wouldn't mind the interruption. The movie was just the excuse for hanging out together—"girl power" was what really mattered. Take, for example, our first Christmas together. We came up with the "Christmas Extravaganza," a reason to dress up for a special date without the necessity of having long-term romances. In order to achieve equality and neutrality, we made careful plans. We budgeted what it would cost for one guy to take out one girl for a night on the town, then the girls spent the same budget on gifts for the gentlemen. After we'd gotten all dressed to the nines, the matches were chosen at random from a hat. (Years later we learned that our wonderful guy friends were more conspiratorial than we ever guessed, but that's another story ...) Looking back on it, Brandon once said, "Most girls put on a dress and, well, it looks like just another girl in a dress. But what makes the Extravaganza so great is that y'all know how to wear a dress!"

Our wild idea turned into an annual event. But one year we were short a girl, of all the crazy things, and as the rest of the ladies gathered to get ready, I scrambled to find a charming dinner date to balance the equation. Prerequisite: she must be as beautiful on the inside as she is on the outside. Jenny, a slender brunette who had grown up in western Iowa, was a perfect fit. So in a flash, we turned our focus on her and created a diva.

After that, Jenny had become one of our own and had rounded out the trio of roommates for our cozy corner room in the sorority house-looking dorm where they all gathered now to watch a movie.

Annika was the first to notice me. "Well, look who decided to show up!" she scolded.

I cozied up to Elisa, hoping that my silly grin would make her smile and forget. "I'm sorry. I'm a horrible friend," I whimpered.

"Well, he must be pretty special," Elisa consoled. "You're one of the most loyal people I know. Of all people, if he can distract you this badly ... well, that's saying something."

"So, you gonna just sit there?" Annika asked slyly. "Or are you going to tell us where you've been?"

My face must have been flushed with emotions, but little was coming out of my mouth. I stammered for something intelligible.

"Well, it just came out of nowhere. I mean, we knew when we started this that we were seriously pursuing the Lord, but, well, I guess according to him, it's been like eighty days."

"You mean he's keeping track? Wow!" Jenny replied, impressed.

"Oh my gosh, have you seen our room?" Annika cut in. "It looks like a flower shop! He's definitely serious."

"I was just waiting for him at his dorm while he talked to his dad. And he came out with this funny look on his face." I replayed the night's event in my mind. "I guess he'd been telling his dad that he could see me being 'the one.' And his dad asked him if he had told me."

"And?" prompted Elisa.

"Well, he just wanted me to know how serious he was about marriage. That he really adores me and is so impressed with how the Lord has brought us together."

"Awww!" squealed all the girls together.

I smiled, but only halfheartedly. "Well, it just seems like I'm suddenly on a racetrack. It's the Indy 500 and we're getting all the green lights from our families and from the Lord. It's a little bit scary."

"Ha!" snorted Jenny. "I'm stuck on the track just trying to get my engine to turn over."

"Yeah, well, I seem to be stuck going round and round and round the track," said Anni with a laugh.

I was rolling as I threw it back on all of them. "When you all finally get married and walk down the aisle, I'm gonna be standing at the back with a big old checkered flag!" With that, we burst into a torrent of giggles as my friends assured me how happy they were for me.

～～ ～

But in a moment, the fairy tale turned sour. My white knight had fallen from his horse. Knights aren't supposed to fall. Heroes aren't supposed to lose. Shortly after his fall, Iglesias' song played continually over the mechanical whir of the machine that was breathing for him. It was as if we believed that hearing his theme song would remind him of what he had to fight for, that he was needed by all of us. Needed by me. No matter how brave he was or how noble, Paul was fragile, just like every one of us. And no magical kiss would revive him.

Now sitting behind the wheel of my car, I feel squashed between my memories and my future. Every day I want to rush to Paul's bedside, but my broken heart knows that Paul and all his love for me would want something better to come from our story. I roll up to a stop sign and engage in my self-indulgent metaphor a little longer. I am at the crossroads. God and I have been wrestling for some time about the direction I should be going. He has been tugging me forward, I have been lingering back. Now is the time to decide.

I hear the squeal of my tires as I hit the gas to move my car forward. It's time.

Surprised to enjoy the familiarity of the city I once so desperately wanted to leave, I speed up, anxious to reach my destination. "I'm home," I call as I walk through the front door. Somehow my parents' home captures the same magical feel that Grandma's house had when I was little.

Suddenly at my feet there is a lonely little whine, and I look down to see an adorable puppy. My mother's handiwork: a six-pound wiggling, long-haired Angel on four legs waiting to come home with me.

"Your new best friend," Mom tells me, smiling.

A two-year-old Yorkshire terrier, her full name is Angelina Little Lady, and she quickly becomes my sidekick. She has just as much personality as I do and she, too, loves to cuddle. With our matching dark hair and tousled blonde tips, we're a crazy pair.

Angel travels home with me where she shares my meals, my couch, and even my pillow. Every night I count on her small form to be lying next to my hip, and early in the morning, when we both look the most scruffy, she is at her cutest.

My mom knew what she was doing by giving me this constant companion. Angel seems to sense when I'm at my worst; any time she hears sobbing, she comes running to sit in my lap. On Sunday afternoons at the park I am no longer alone; strangers coo over my bundle of joy. To be loved so devotedly and completely by this little creature seems to be exactly what the doctor ordered. In the midst of all my chaos, when I don't think I can stick with my commitment to move forward, those lively trusting eyes look up at me and give me a reason to get up and head out into the world.

Going out into the world sometimes means staying holed up in front of my computer where I write—for hope, for obedience, for Paul, for myself, for others. It's confusing sometimes, writing my story. It has no happy ending. Not in this life at least. This reality seems to fly in the face of "Christian writing" as I know it. Our story is messy. Paul is not dead and communing with the Lord, but he isn't alive and living with me, miraculously restored. We are caught in a cruel reality that seems anything but hopeful.

Still, God had been a central character in our love story even to the end. Our story is nothing noble or supernatural, but it does hold a miracle. Two miracles, in fact. The first happened quietly here on earth: A gentle God stood by an almost widow and nurtured her faith even when she felt forgotten. He ministered to her wounds and brought healing. I have seen doctors attempt to heal the body, and even succeed, but I know firsthand that only God can truly heal the heart. The second miracle hasn't happened yet, but I am already thankful—thankful for the day that Paul stands whole and full of laughter, the day all of us are whole, standing before our Creator. It is the hope of this day that keeps me moving.

For now it is enough that God sustains me each day. As I write, I see how profoundly my faith has changed. I don't have a plan for my writing, and at times I feel foolish. But a strange sense of peace has filled me and sustains me as I pour out my heart. I have no idea what will come of my scribbling. In my audacious moments I give that responsibility to God. But if I am able to share my journey, the lessons that guided me through doubts, the God who comforted me when I felt so alone, it seems a sacred heritage to pass on. I dare to hope that my words will go places I can't go, that his truth will bring healing to others lost in the valley.

# EPILOGUE

*Whatever our souls are made of, his and mine are the same.*
Emily Brontë

The first time I saw Sarah, it was impossible not to be moved by her words and her heart as she shared with others her journey of faith, doubt, and sustained trust. She was giving her testimony to our New Covenant Bible Church family about how the Lord had sustained her through the tragedy of losing Paul and how her understanding of God had grown. Even as her words were broken off by tears, there was a powerful strength in her spirit. In spite of all the tragedy she had endured, I was moved by her honesty, and it was obvious that her only motive was to communicate hope with other hurting people. As she spoke, I could instantly see that God had bestowed an extra measure of grace in Sarah. In the middle of her own pain she understood there were others who were lost in the middle of terrible circumstances, looking for God and wondering if they had been forgotten. She was able to speak from a deep fountain of compassion.

As the son of an African preacher, I grew up listening to powerful and moving testimonies, but what impressed me about Sarah was that she didn't try to smooth over the hard questions or explain them away. She simply pointed out how God had been tender and attentive. I will never forget the sense of peace that seemed to surround her. You couldn't help but see that she was very close to God and very important to him.

After the service, a mutual friend introduced me to Sarah's parents, Joan and Blane, and I learned that Sarah's background strangely paralleled my own. While Sarah was ensconced in Chicago, I spent the majority of my time getting to know her parents as we ministered together at New Covenant Bible Church and to other internationals in our area, especially fellow Africans.

≈ ≈

My earliest childhood memories involved travel to different countries, and I grew up with parents who followed the Lord wherever he led. Since my father was studying to be a leader in the Evangelical Church in Chad, we always knew we would return one day, but at the age of eleven I was far more American than African. I loved my home country; however, education presented a challenge as I was unfamiliar with the French language or the school system. I was homeschooled for a year and also spent nearly half a year in France to become fully bilingual. When I was entering my last year of junior high school, unknown to Sarah or me at the time, both of our parents were looking into Rift Valley Academy, a boarding school in Kenya where Sarah did eventually attend. To this day I wonder what it would have been like had I actually enrolled, but as always, God knew I had much more growing up to do before he introduced us officially. Instead I remained in Chad for another year before landing on the other side of Africa at a boarding school in Burkina Faso.

Following my sophomore year of high school, I moved from Burkina Faso to Seattle, where I completed high school while living with an aunt and cousins. A few years later, after graduating from a college in Wisconsin, I moved to Cedar Rapids, Iowa, for my first position. Only months before Paul's accident, I began attending the same church Sarah had grown up in.

Over time I became more and more involved with New Covenant Bible Church and have become very much at home there. So it didn't surprise me when I was invited along with good friends of mine to Sarah's family's home one evening for dinner. What did surprise me was Sarah. I didn't expect to see her there since she lived in Chicago. But when I saw her I lost my breath and my heart started pounding. As the dinner progressed I kept telling myself, "This is too incredible: She is smart, beautiful, and she's had similar experiences living in various countries in Africa." I was more nervous than I had ever remembered being, and to hide it, I just tried not to look at her. Not knowing what Paul and Sarah's situation was after the accident, I took it as a friendly dinner getting to know Sarah's family and Sarah better.

I continued to run into Sarah with her parents when she was home and we would talk, but not in depth. She gave me her contact information and even though I wanted to talk with her, I didn't have a peace about it. I would take out her card and contemplate whether to contact her so often that finally I stuck it in my desk at work. *Lord*, I thought, *this is too amazing to be for me. If this is really from you, you're going to have to make it happen*. With that, I was filled with a sense of peace and gave it back to God; patient, but never really believing it would lead to anything.

⤝ ⤞

Weeks turned into months and the realization set in that Sarah was living in Chicago. I convinced myself that the distance was too far for comfort. I completely enjoyed the family that God had created in Cedar Rapids, but I knew that my wife and partner would have to be someone who would understand the unique experiences and multiple cultures that made up my life. I had remarked time and time again that I would never meet someone like this in Iowa.

Finally I gave it all over to God and committed several mornings to praying about my future spouse and the spouses of my siblings. Again, I was filled with peace, being content even when the future seemed so unknown.

As I settled in Cedar Rapids, I became more and more involved with the local church. A couple years after meeting Sarah for the first time, I found myself volunteering to sell books at an event in town. I was surprised to see Sarah in town in the middle of the week and even more surprised to hear that she had just moved back. Before I could get my mind around this change in fortune, a customer at the book table distracted me. When I looked up again, she was gone.

A few months later I finally met up with her again at a friend's house, and this time we talked. After she walked away that night, I was filled with a sense of urgency. Without hesitation, I sent her an email telling her how great it had been seeing her and that I really did want to get to know her better. I kept throwing the ball back into her court. I knew there was something incredible about her and about how I felt when I was with her, but I didn't want to rush her or overwhelm her with what I was thinking. For our first date we met at the local IMAX theatre to watch a *Stomp* show about dance from around the world. When I looked over at her in the dark, it hit me how amazing she was, and I knew this was the beginning of something beautiful.

On my birthday I proposed to the most wonderful, godly woman I have ever met and received the best birthday gift ever when she said yes. I knew God had prepared us for each other even though the path seemed extremely long at times. And though we had officially dated for only a short period of time, because I spent the last few years getting to know her through her parents and the hand of providence God had on our lives, it seems as if I have known her all my life. It is a blessing to have Sarah as my wife, and I am eternally grateful to my heavenly Father for having the wisdom and foresight to weave our stories together for his glory.

Nate

# ACKNOWLEDGMENTS

Thank you to:

My father, who saw something whole in all the pages and tenderly gathered them together. My mother, who tirelessly dropped everything whenever I needed someone to help me edit, whose red pen was always on the ready. You never let me settle for anything, but you heard my voice and protected my unique perspective. Both of you are the reason that I could have faith in my own words. On top of everything you've given me, you believed in my gift when I thought I had nothing left to give.

Angela Scheff, who discovered this book, believed in it, and poured so much time and heart into it. Your commitment to this text showed me that it was possible for something good to come out of the wreckage.

Becky Shingledecker, who patiently brought form and grace to this collection of emotion.

The Zondervan staff that committed to the "What's In Your Head?" contest. Thank you for believing in the undiscovered voices.

Naomi Casteel Thompson, my counselor and now my friend, you walked me through questions no one else understood, taught me how to embrace my grief, and how to live again.

Vernon and Marlys Awes, you were literally a gracious godsend, and being taken under your wing in the early days gave me a place to feel safe and a reason to smile. Out of the ugliness, your influence and your home were always such a bright spot. It's an honor to call you "my other grandparents."

PIECES *of* GLASS

Ted Humphrey, thank you for investing in me and believing in me.

At Wheaton College:

Dr. Kenneth Chase, for introducing me to Paul and the power of narrative, two of the most precious gifts of my life.

Dr. Ellyn Grosch, for your hospitality and your strength after the accident. You showed me what I was capable of.

Dr. Robert O'Conner for the chance to write my first book.

The Pickering family and your wonderful bookstores.

My incredible, colorful friends. You have stood beside me every step of the way and forgive me when I drop off the face of the planet in the name of writing.

Dana, whose adventure is just beginning. You have been so generous when my life needed so much time and attention. You are an incredible man of God and I can't wait to see what God has in store for you.

Nate, from our very first date you have believed in my writing and have made it a priority in our lives. It's an honor to share my life and my faith with you. In our new love I have found a place for the old, and that takes an incredible person.